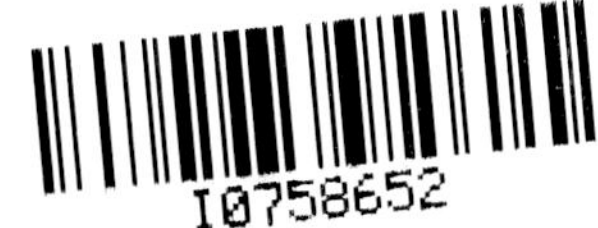

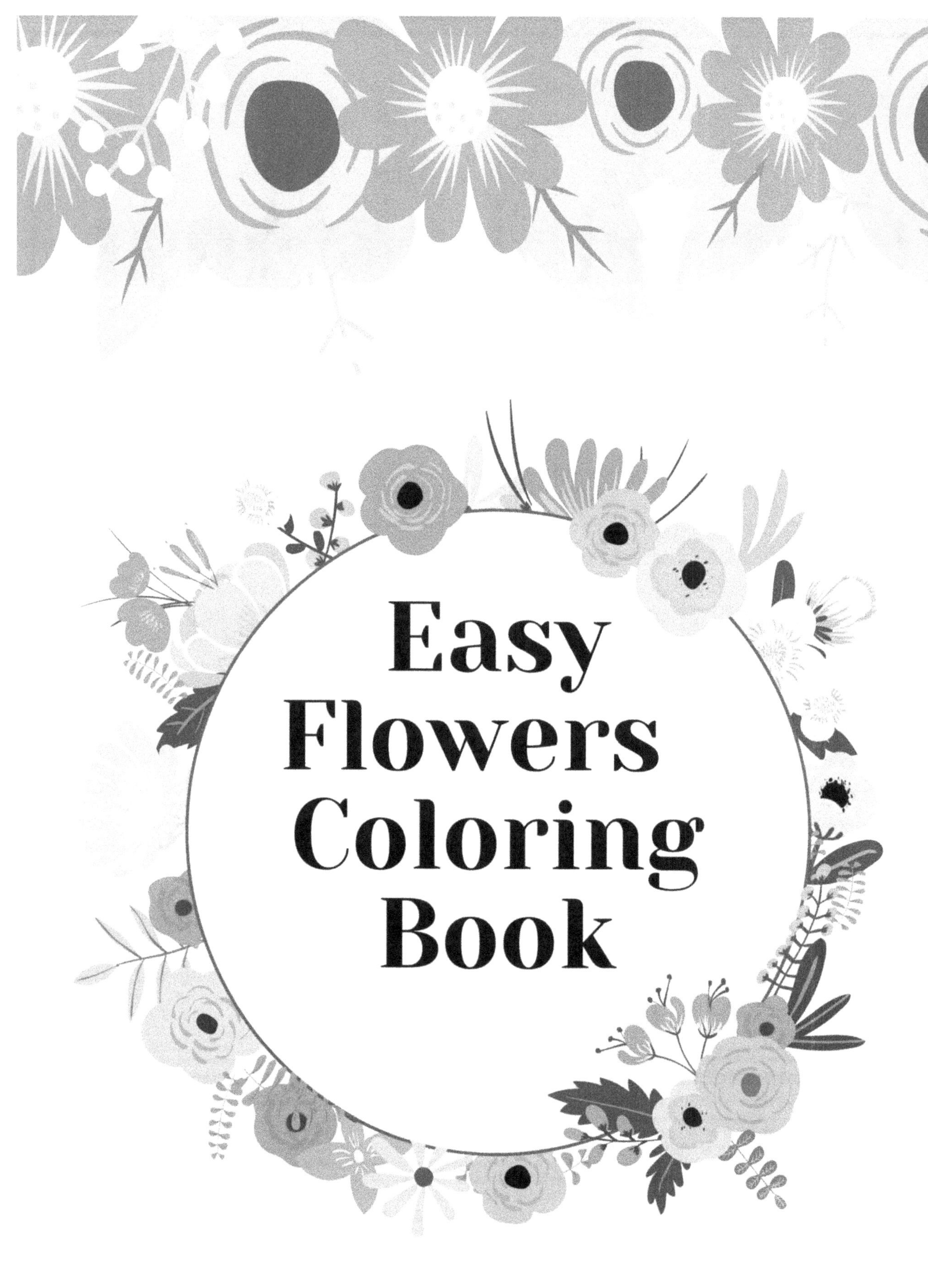

Easy
Flowers
Coloring
Book

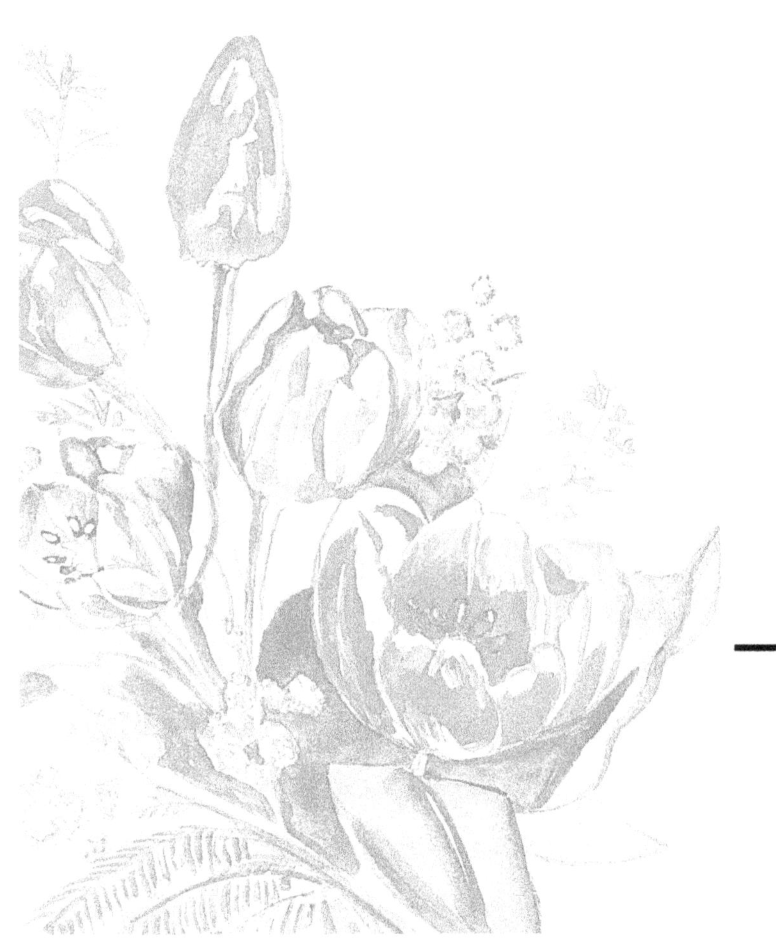

THIS BOOK
COLORING
BY

____

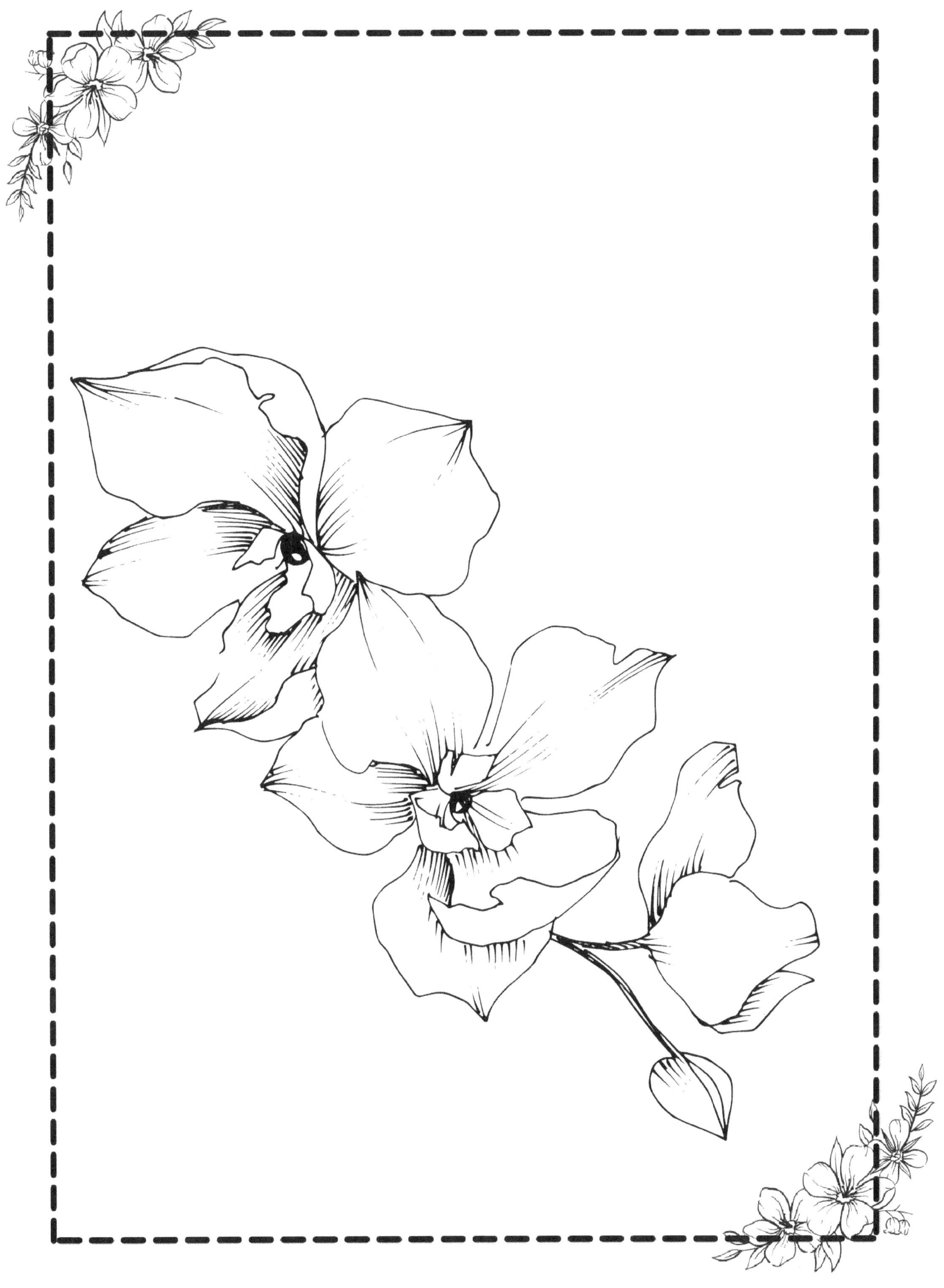

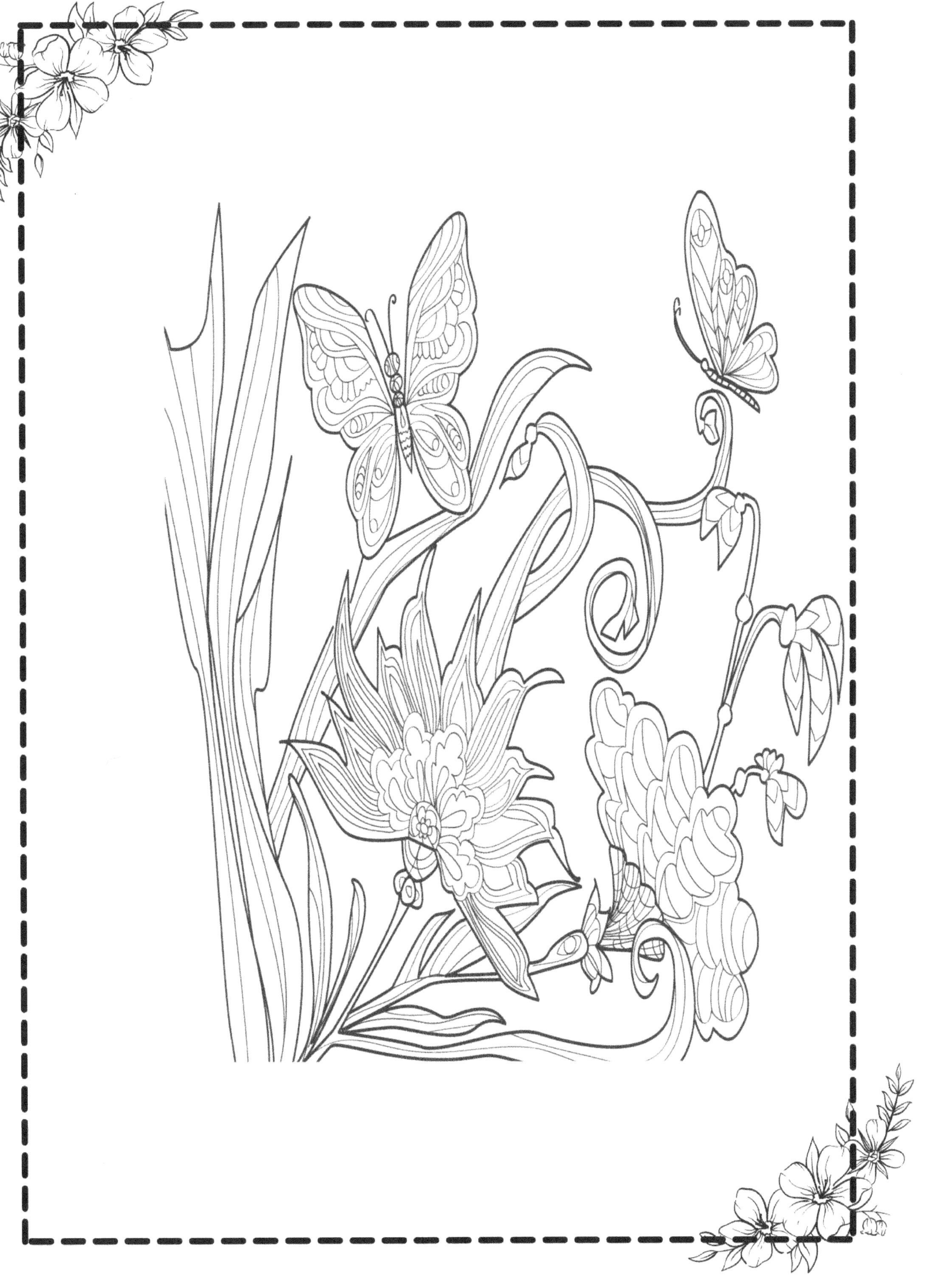

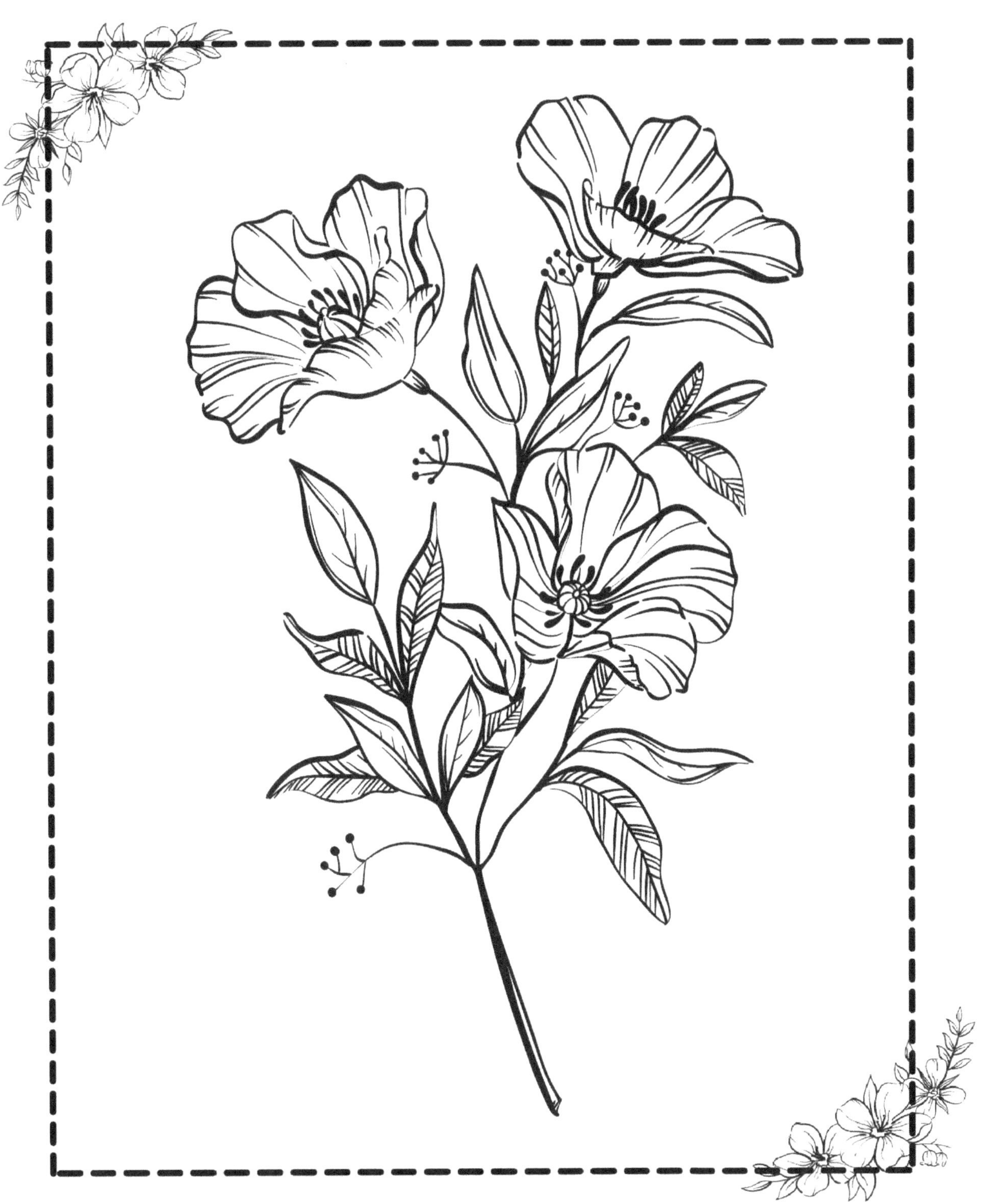

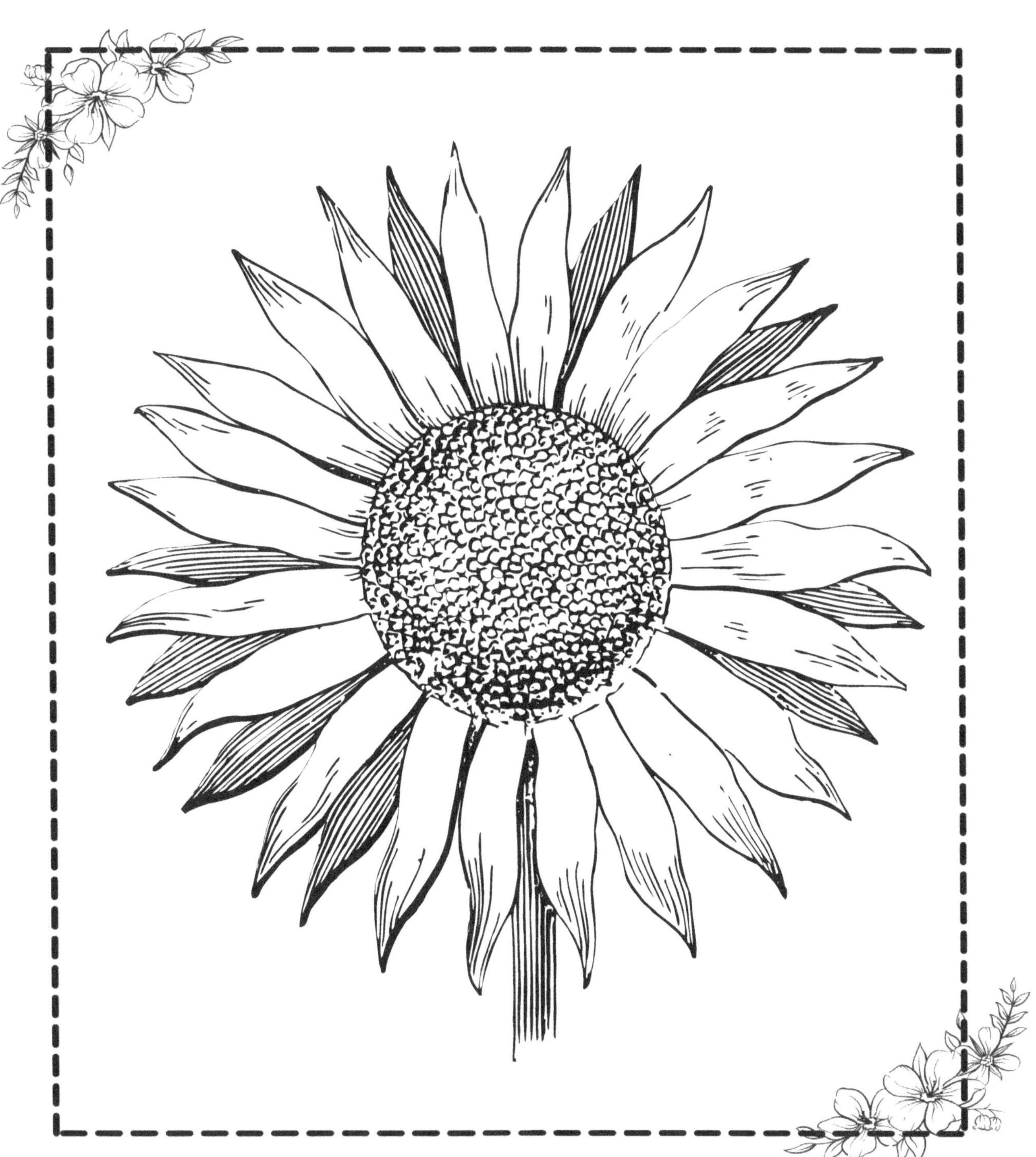

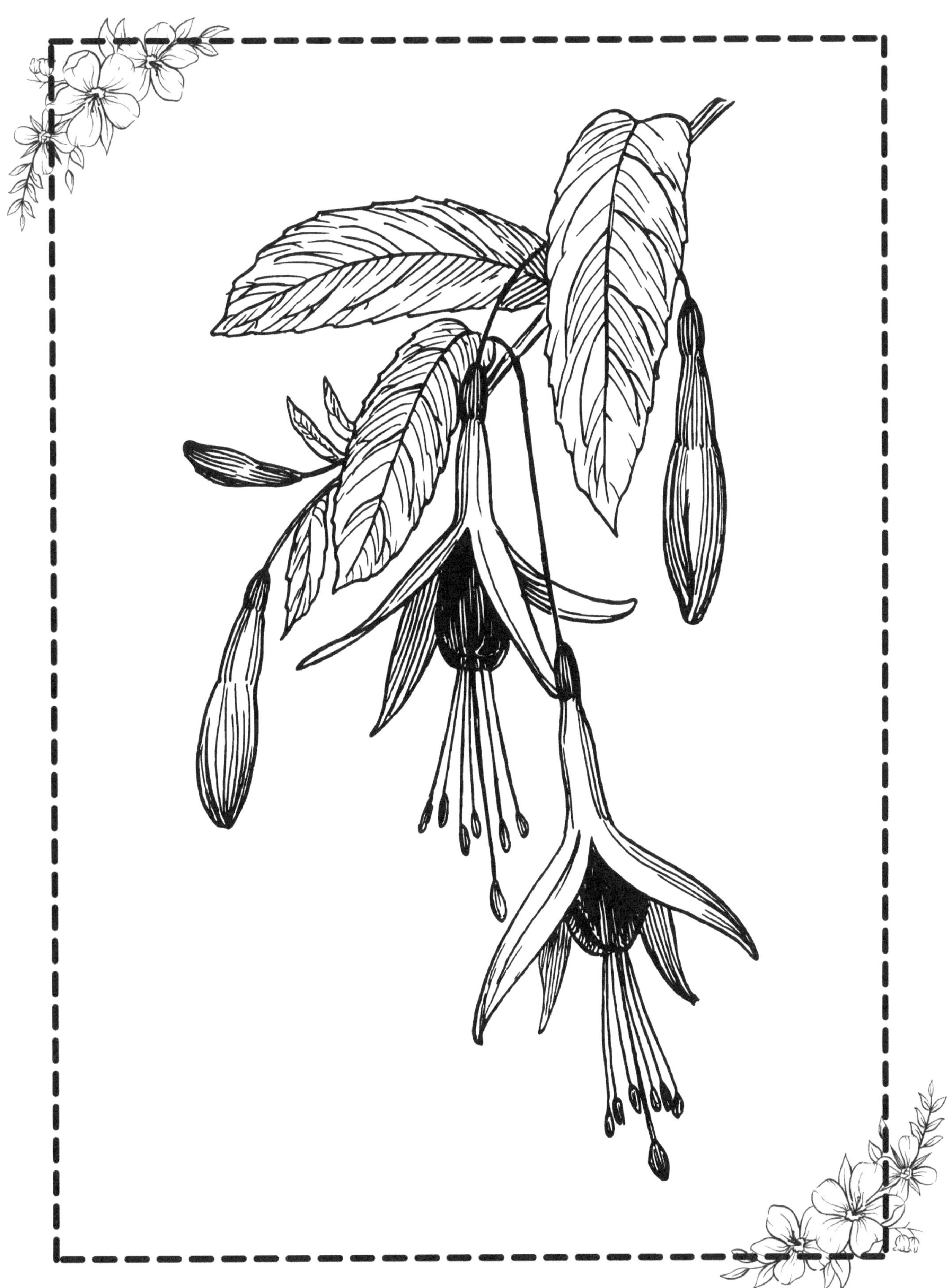

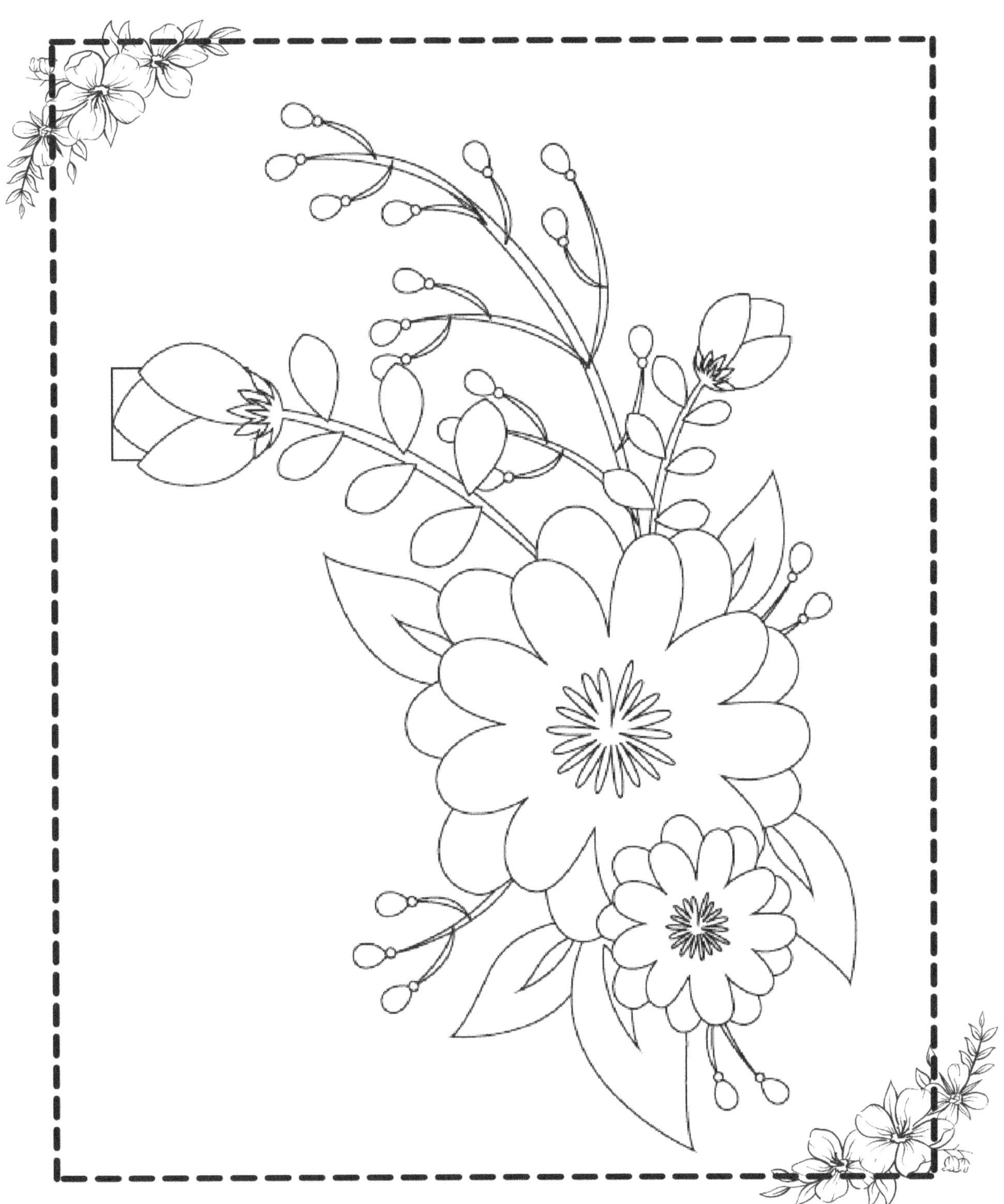

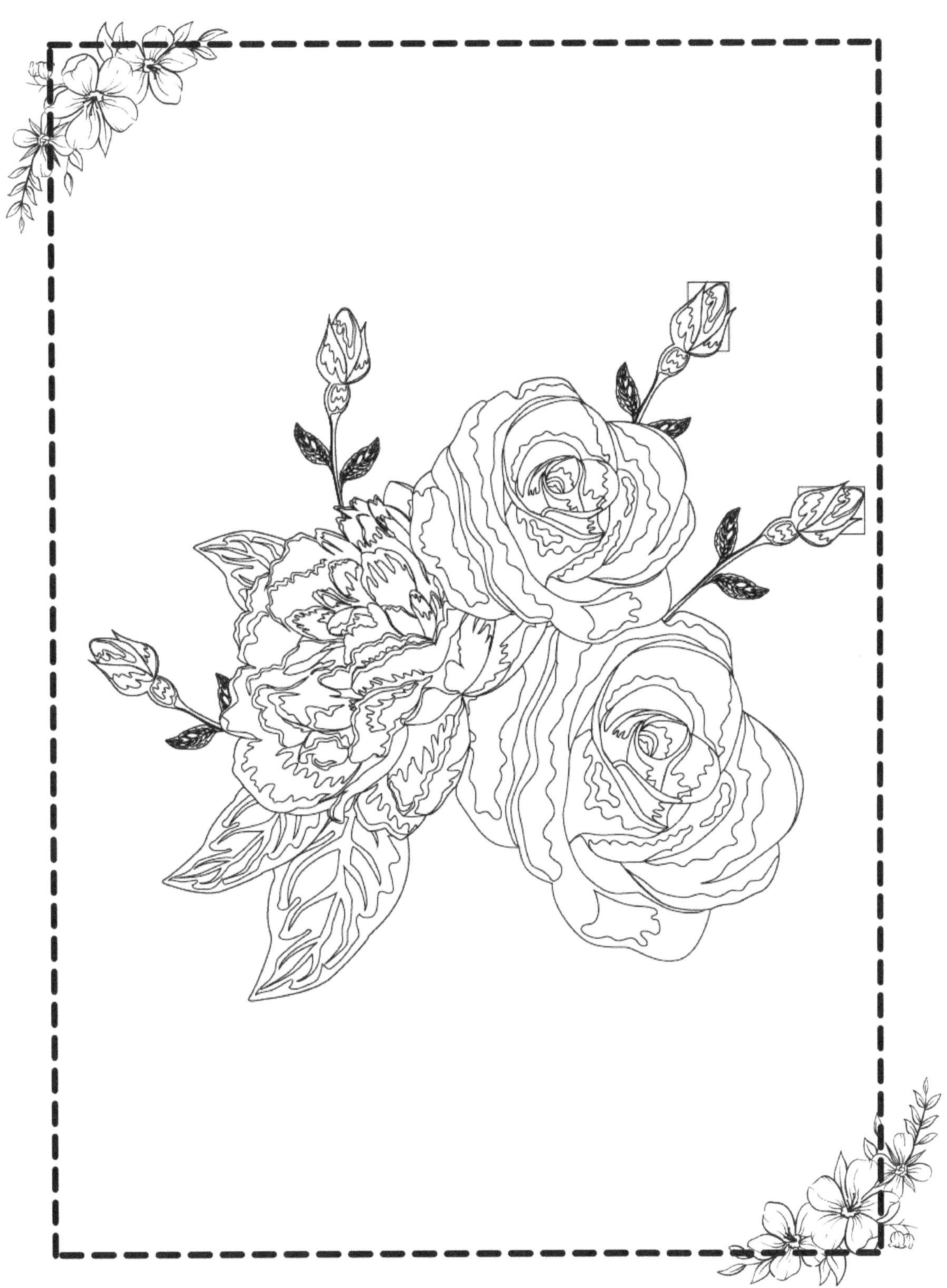

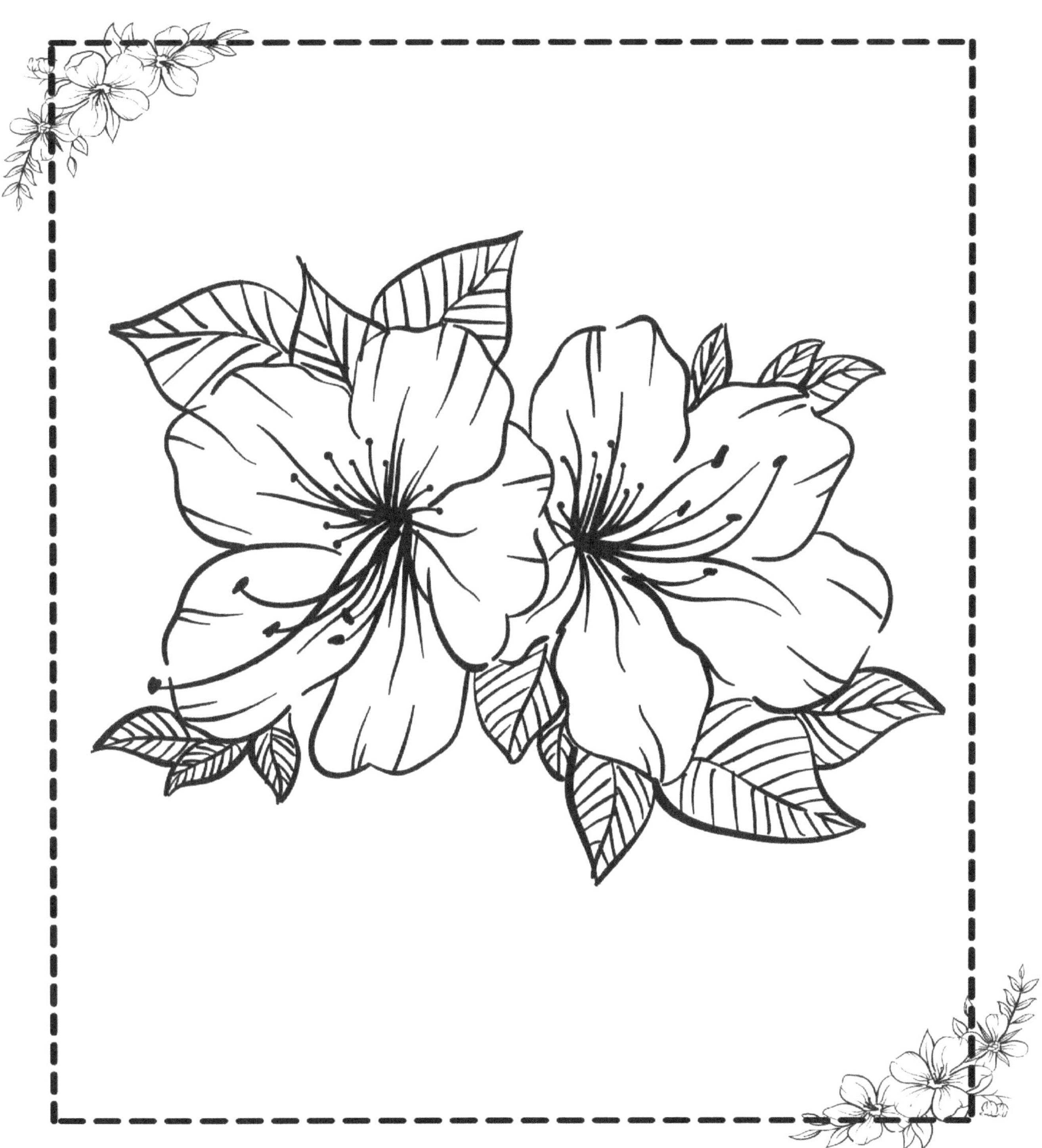

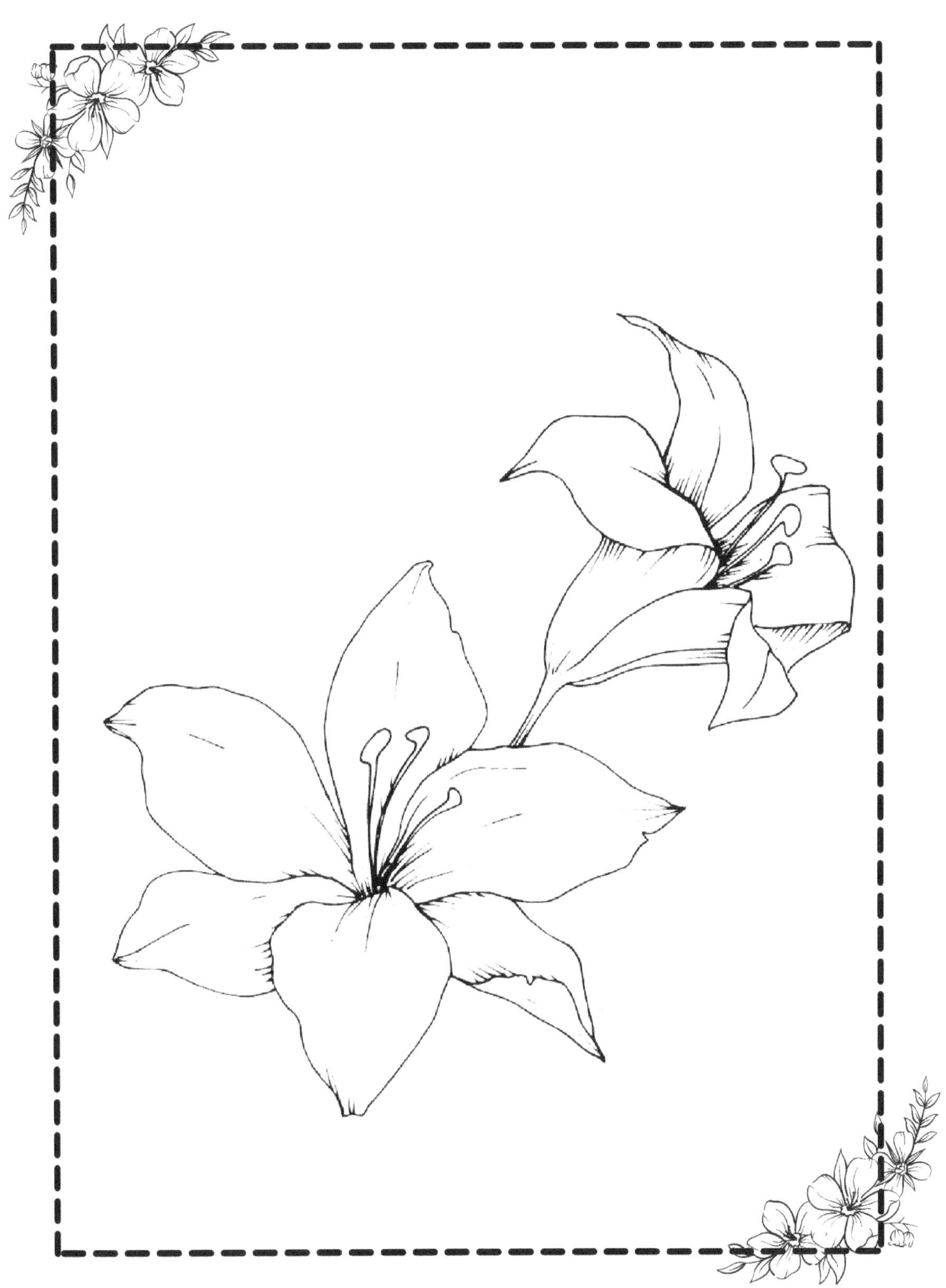

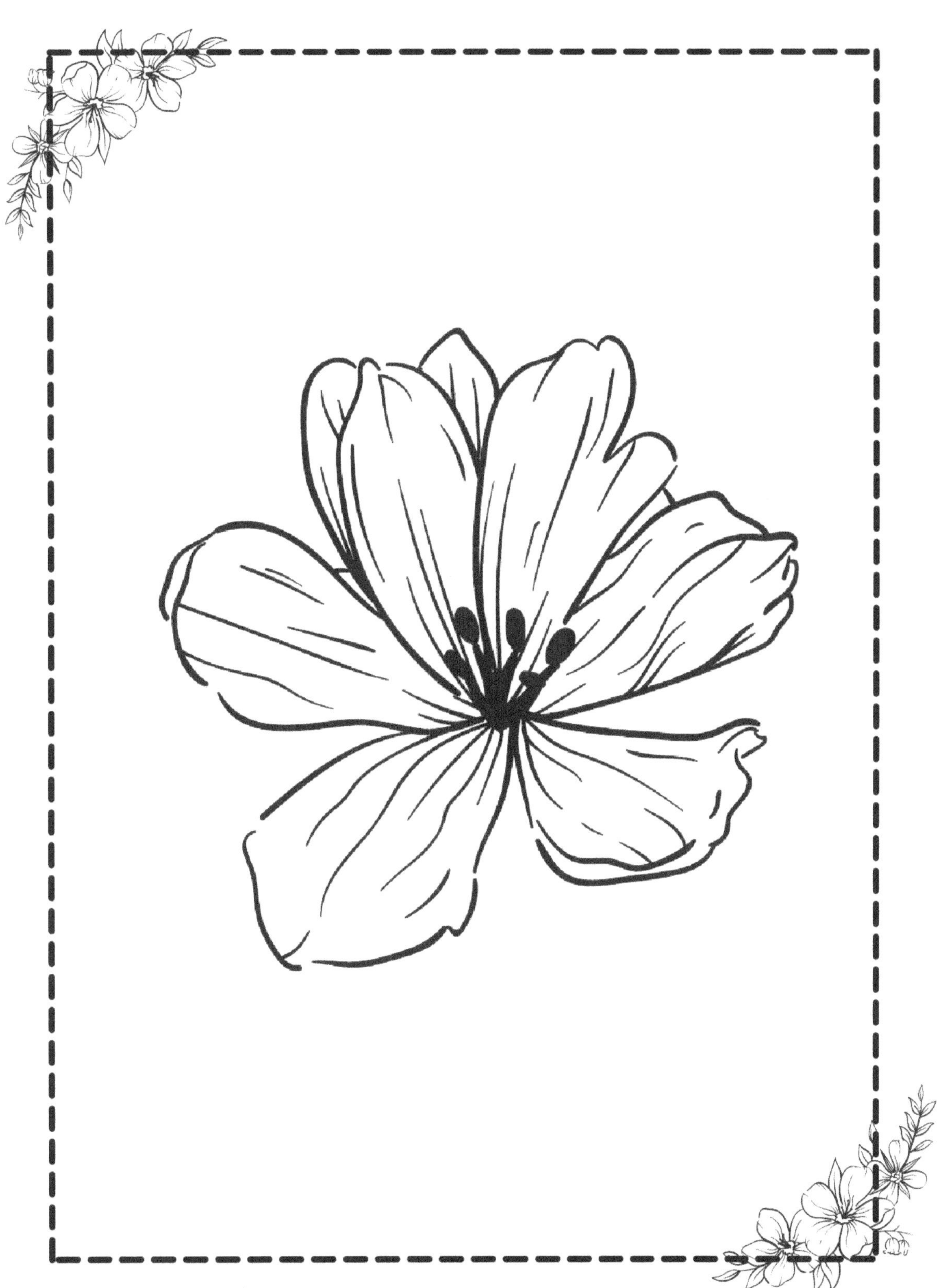

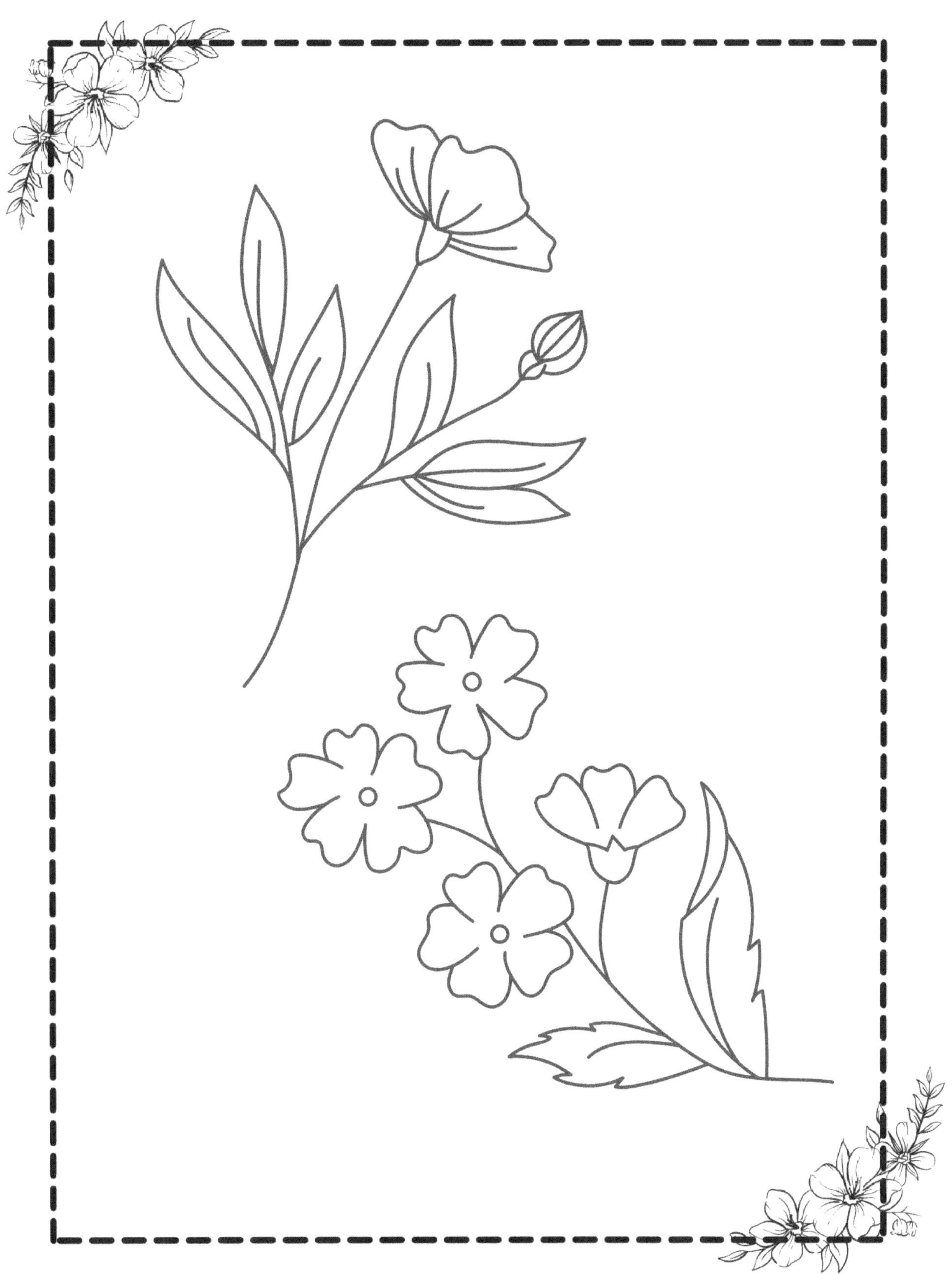

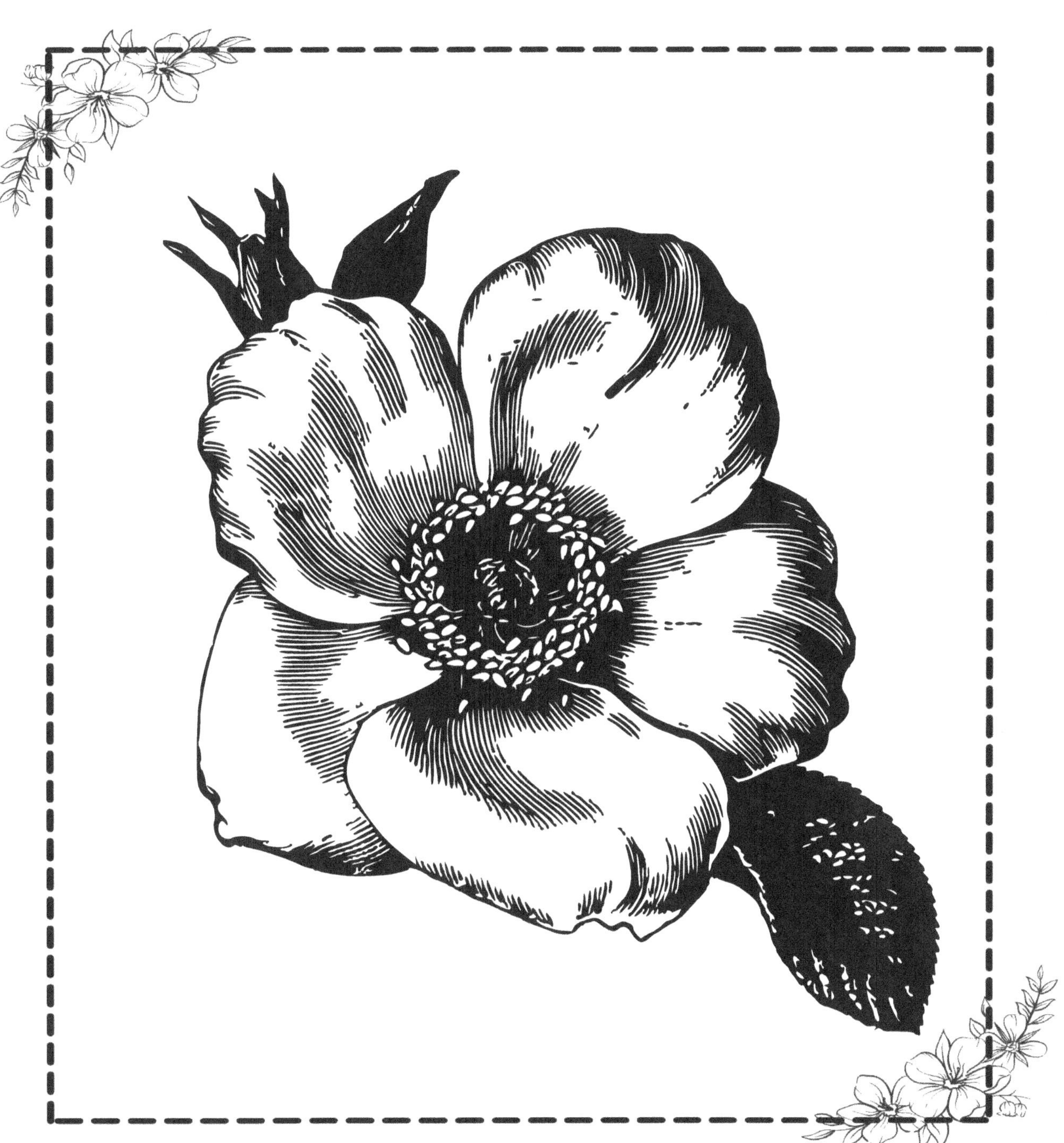

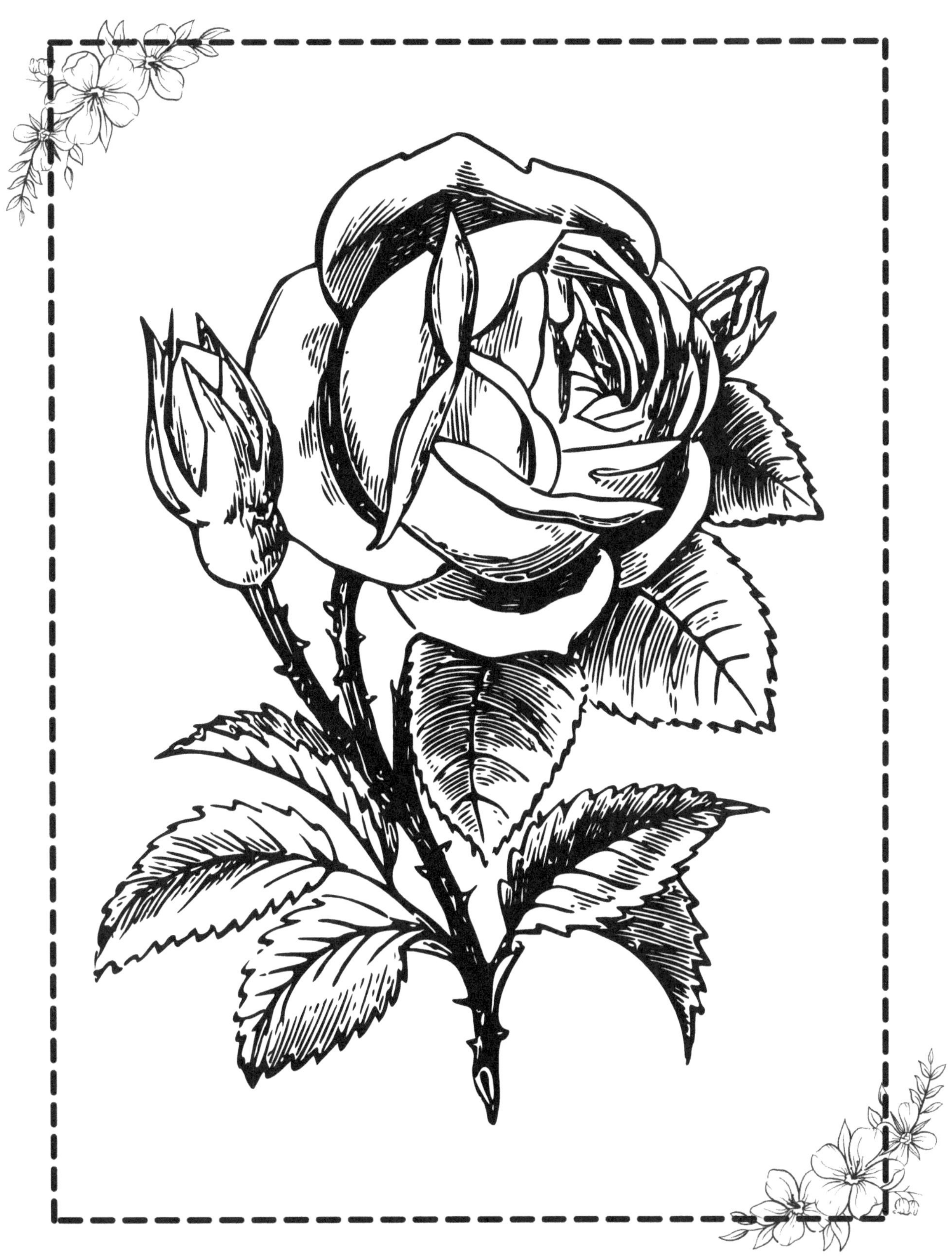

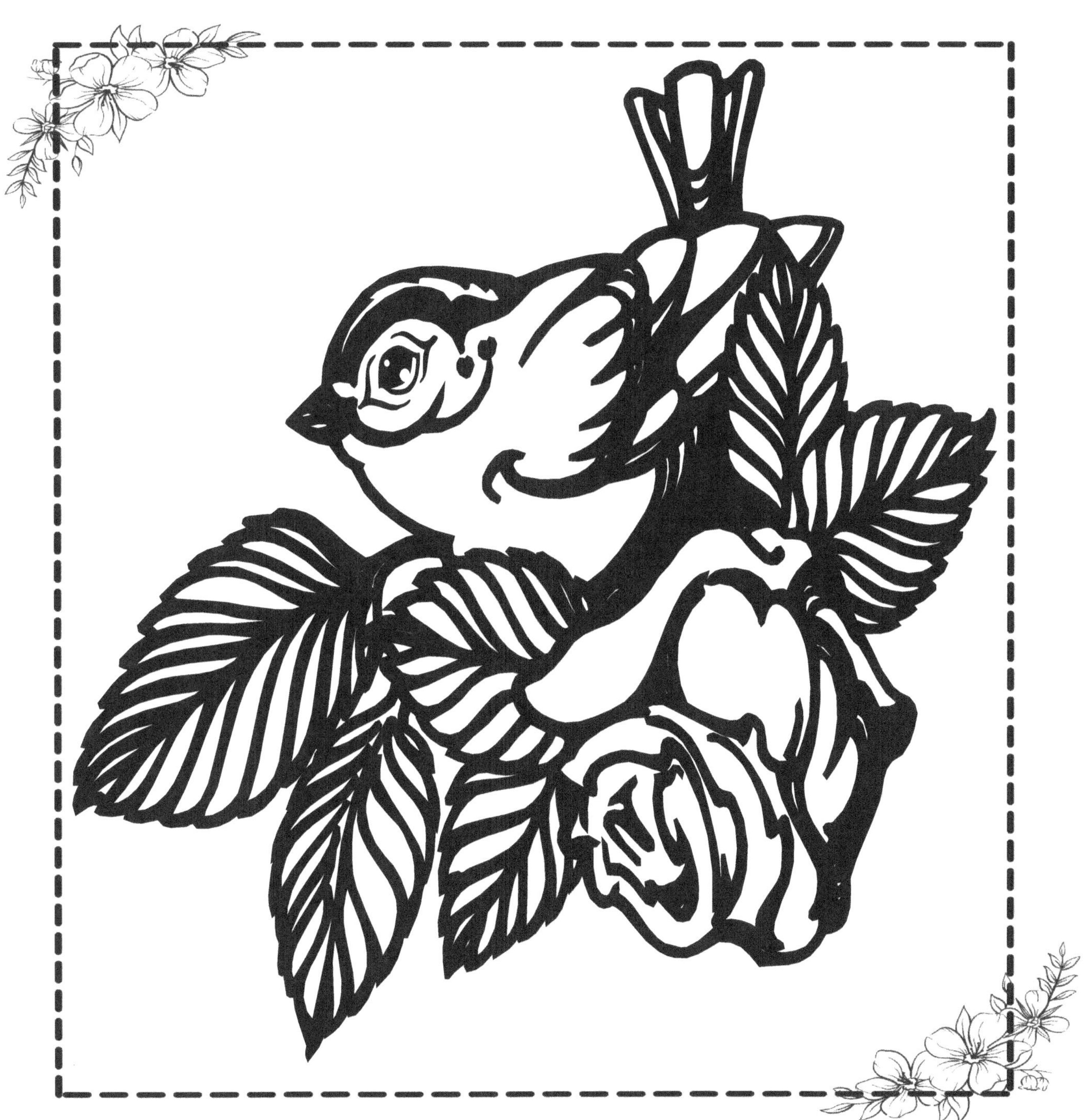

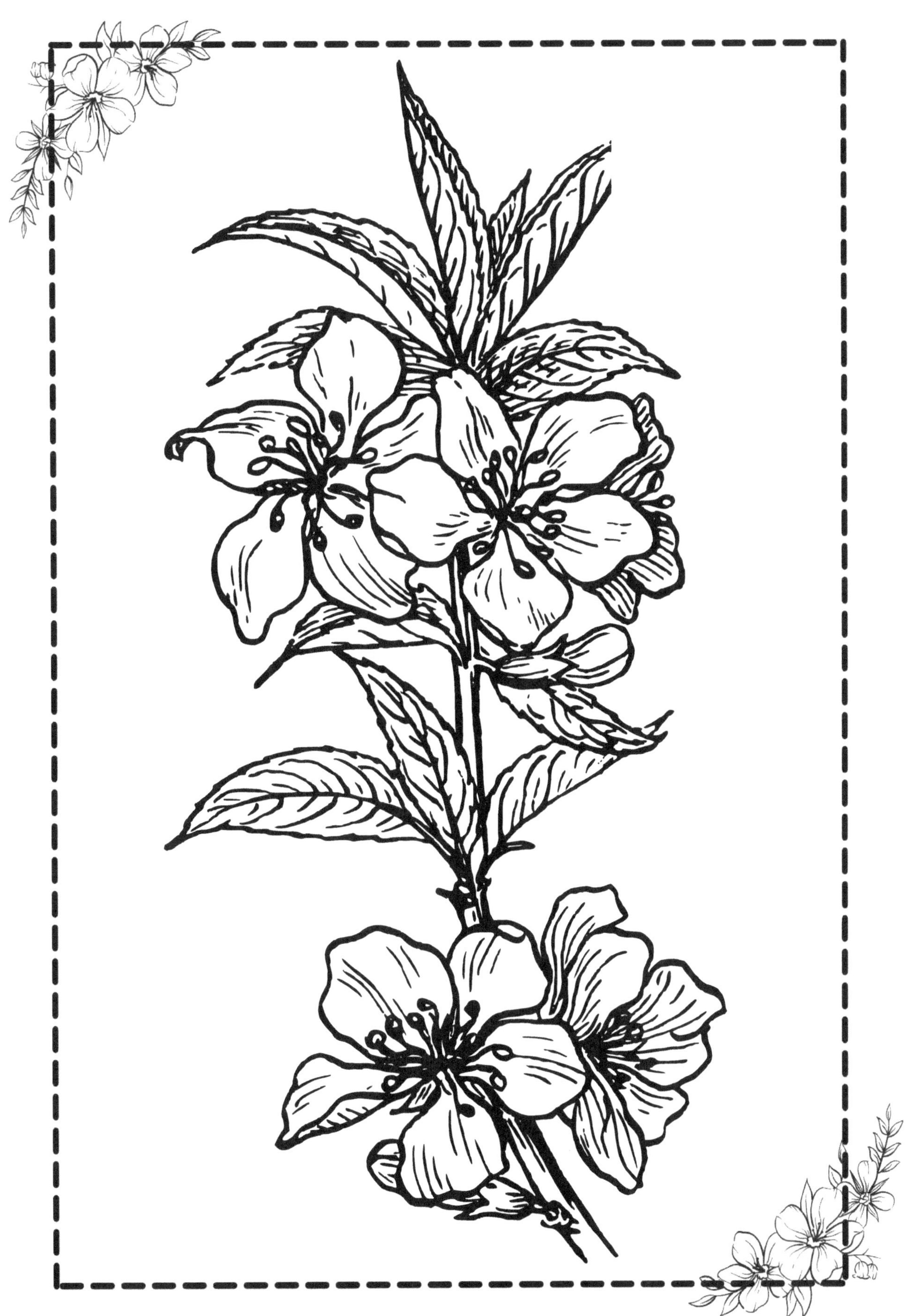

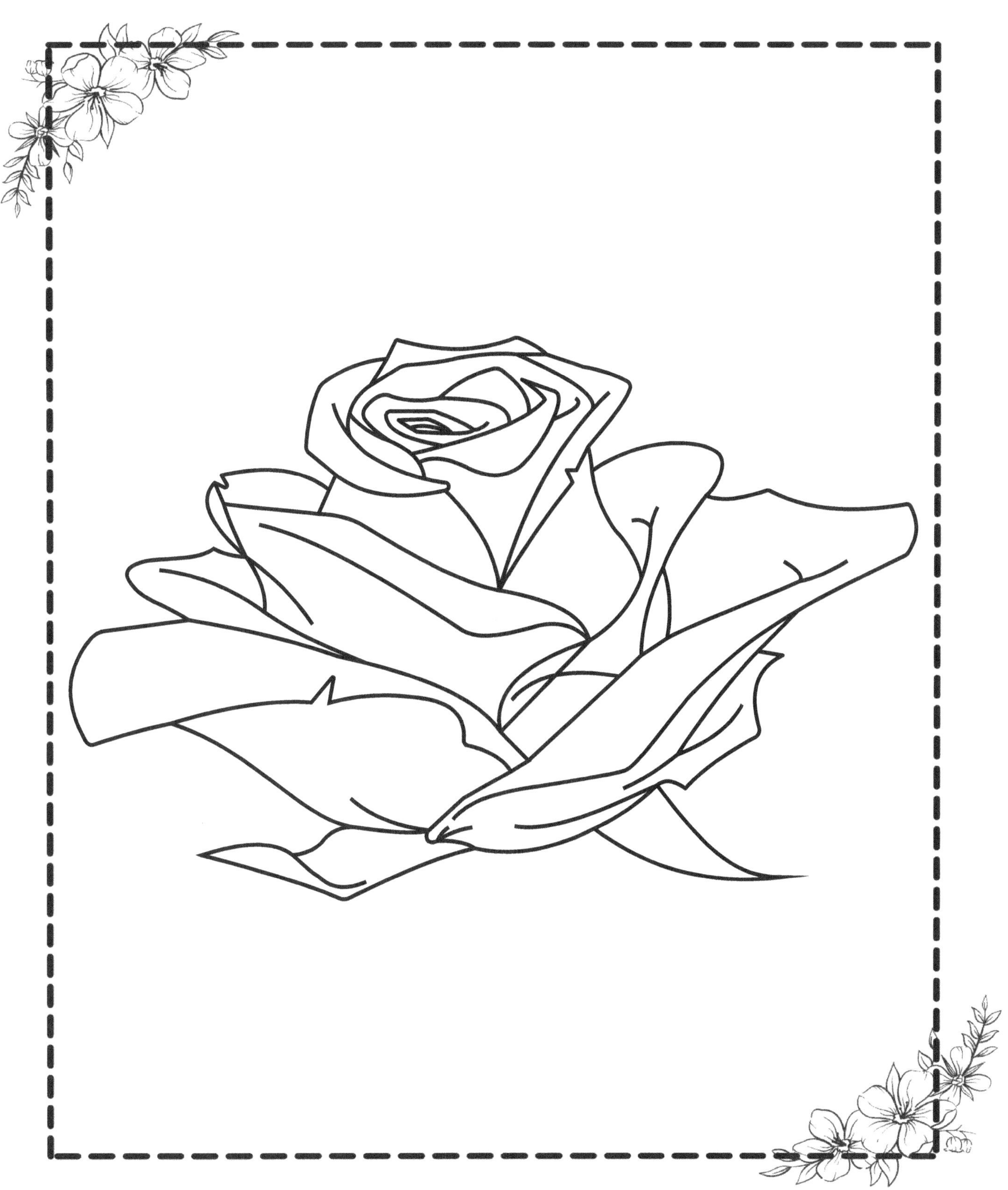

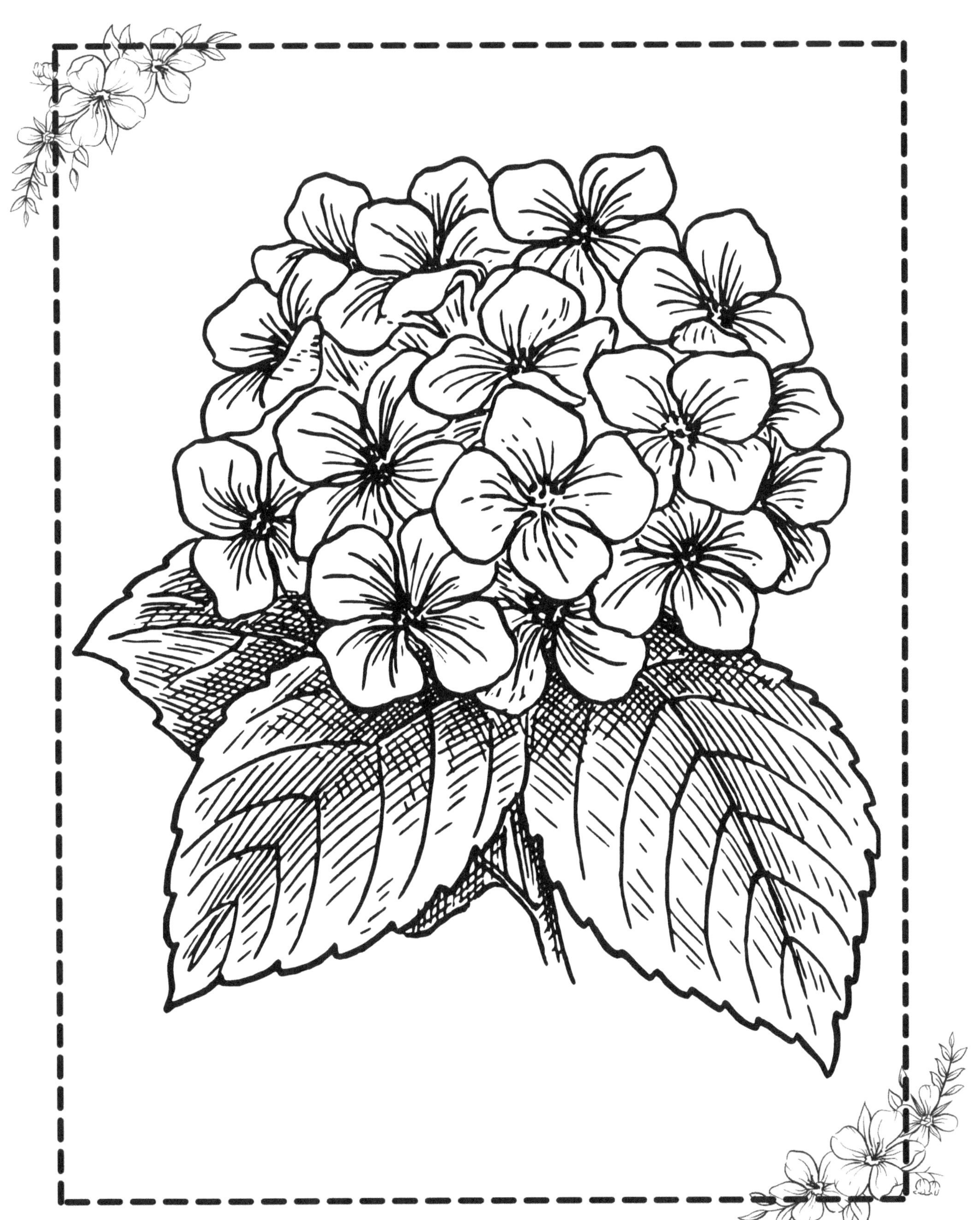

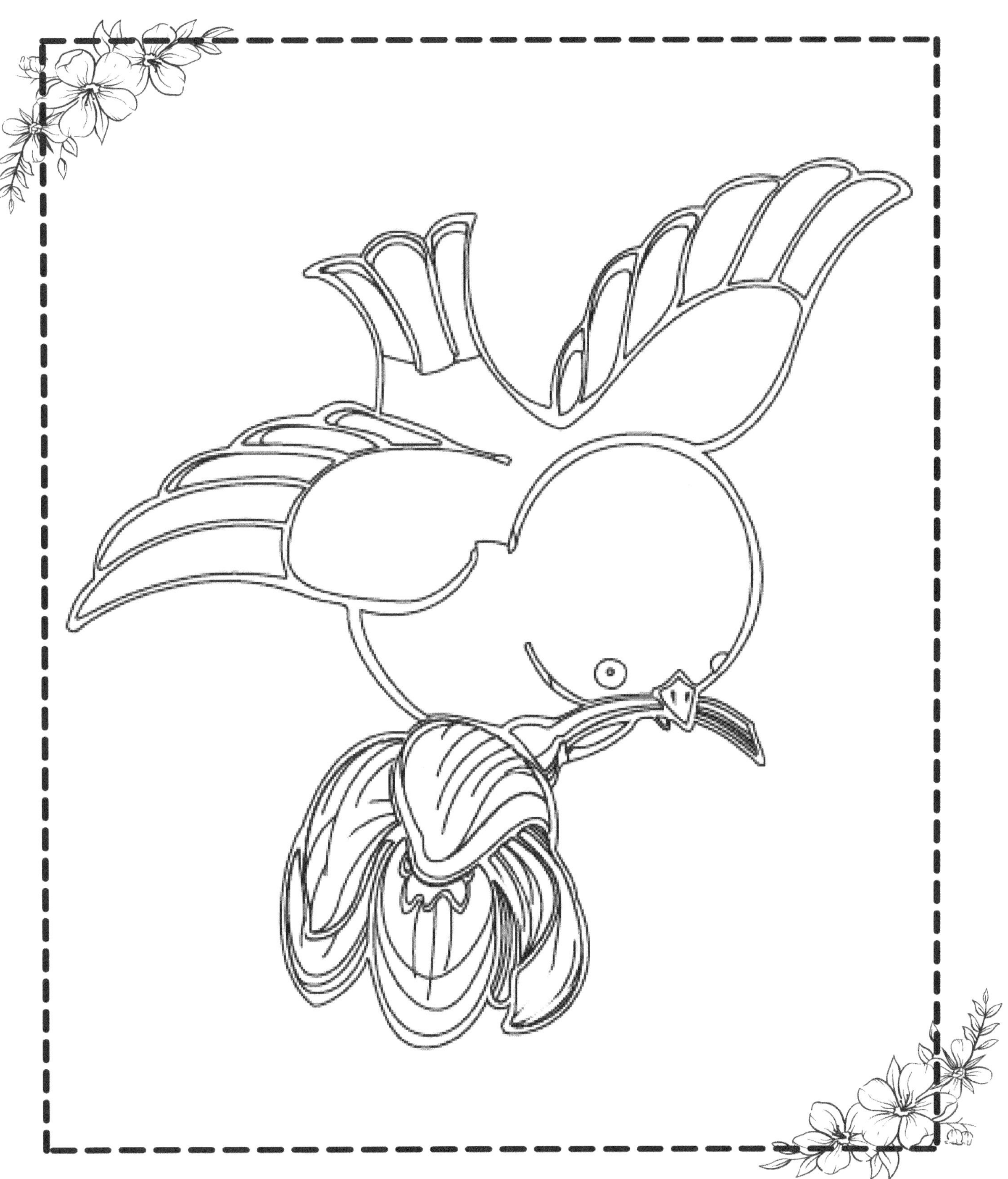

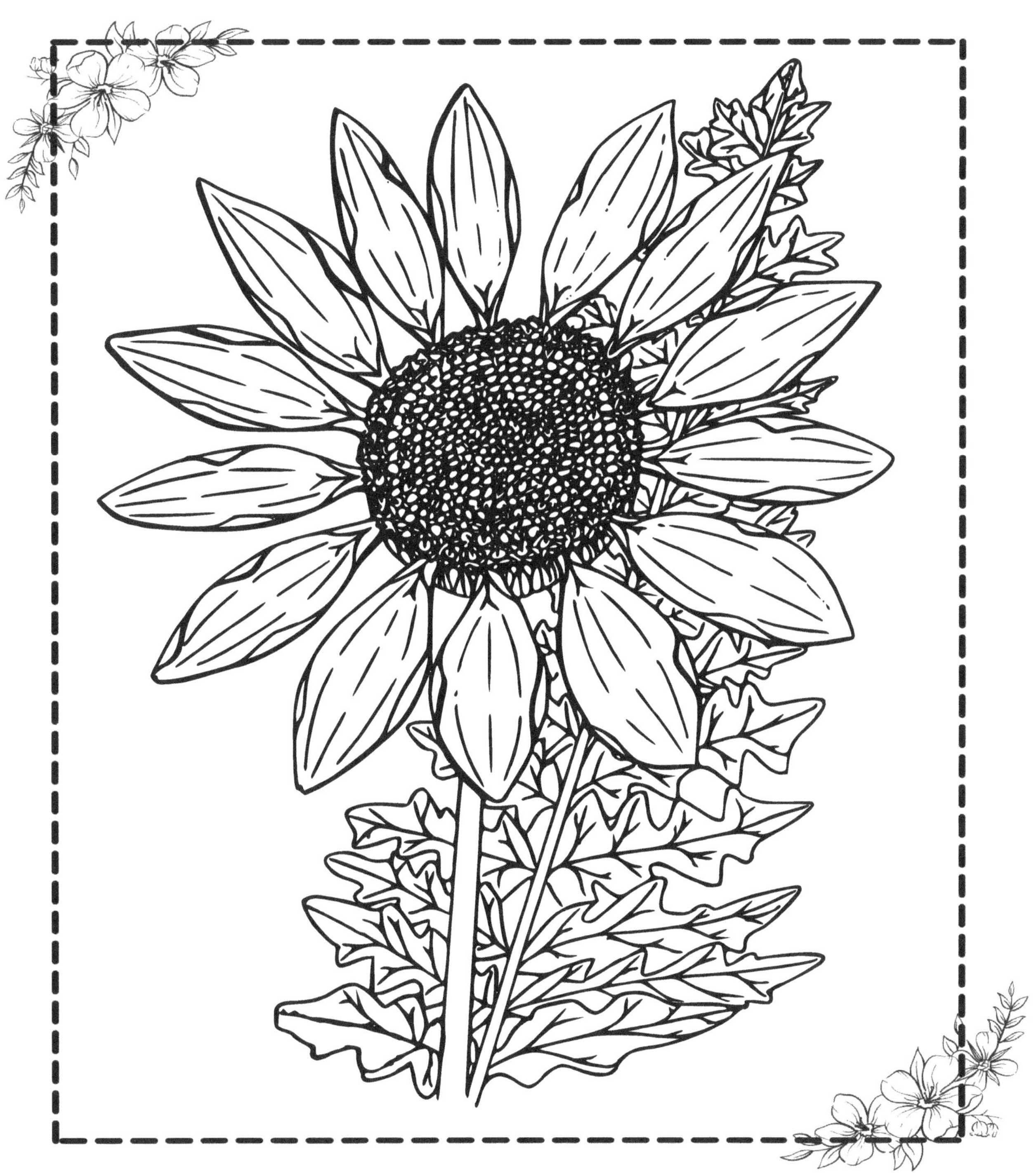

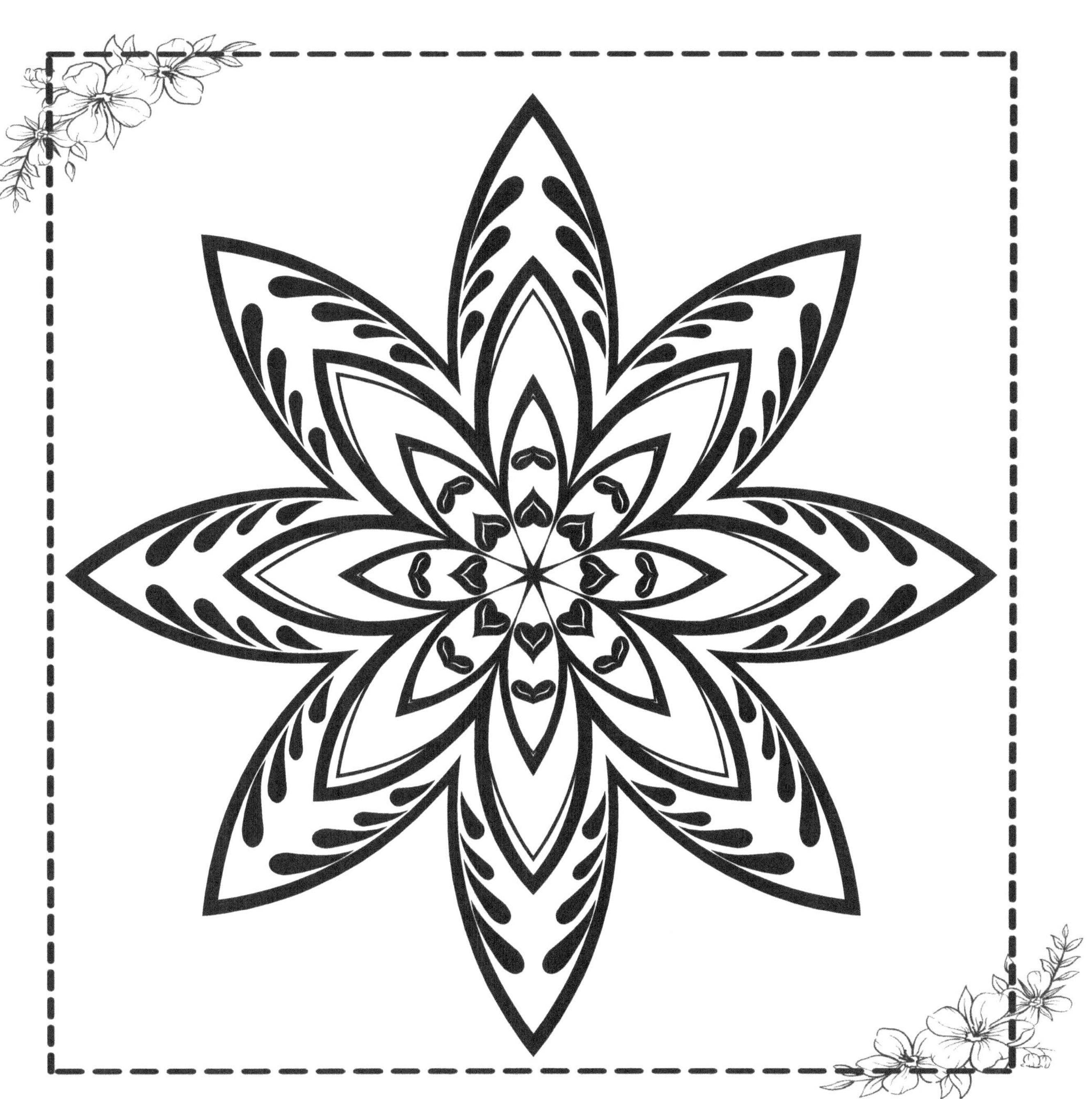

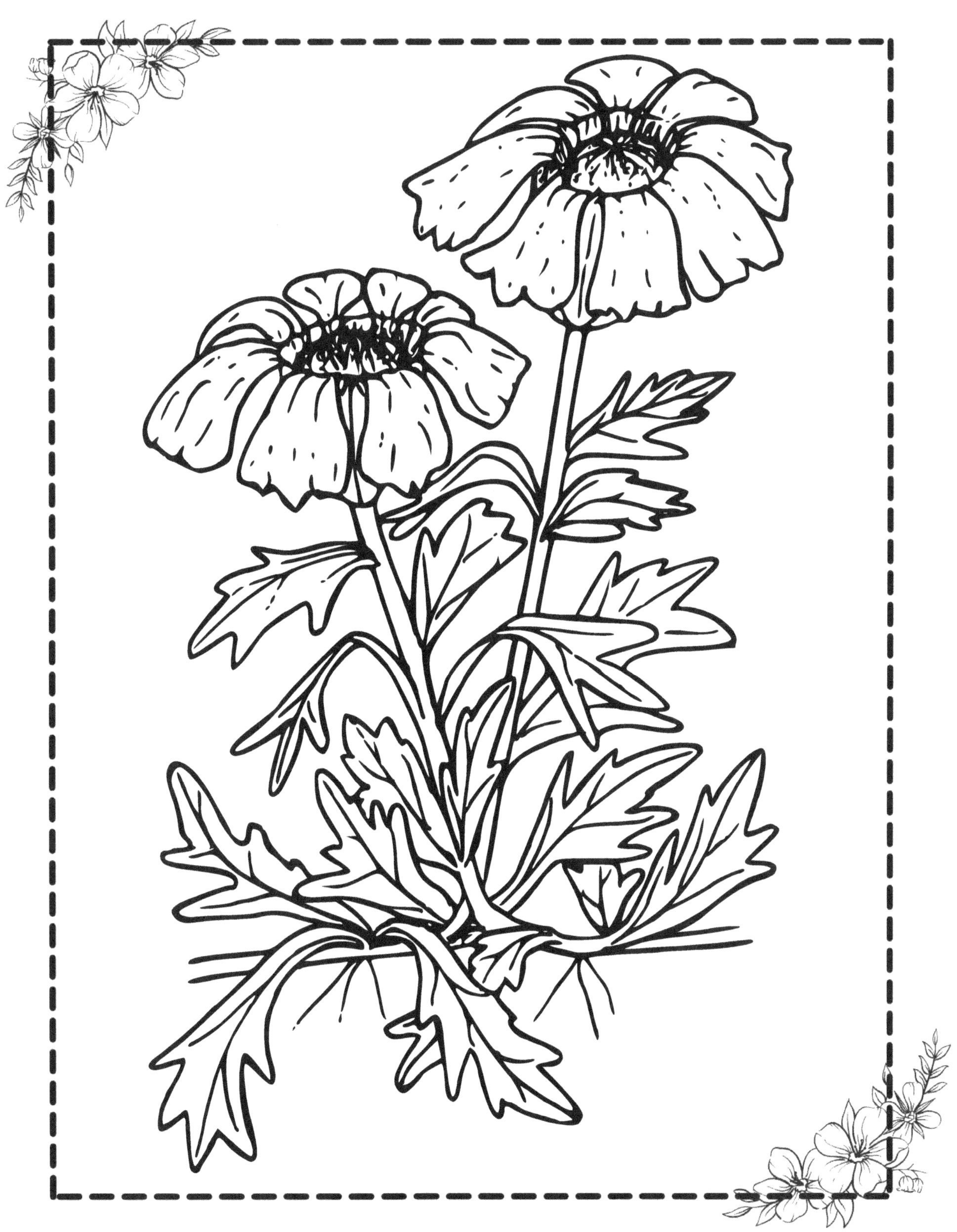

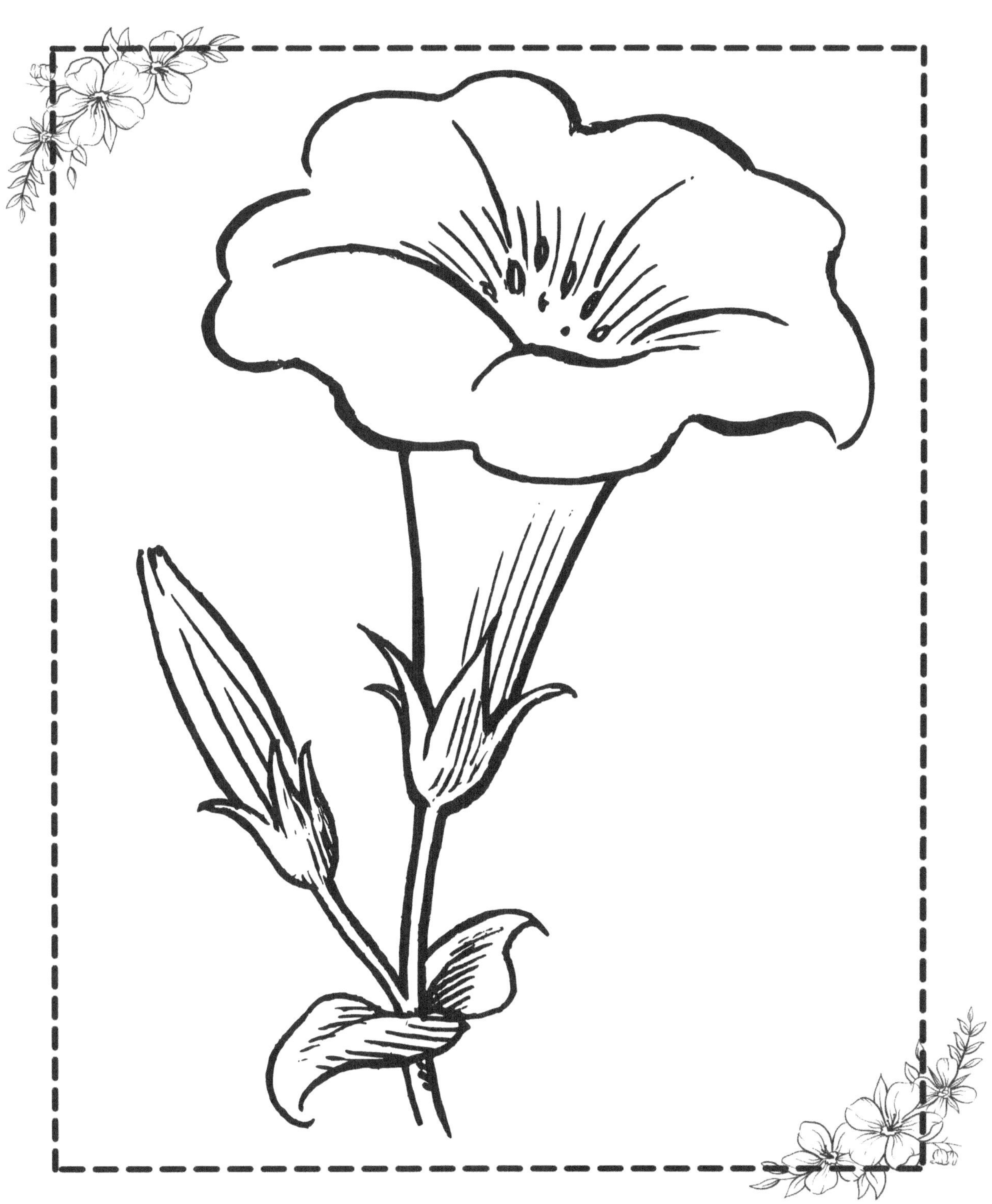

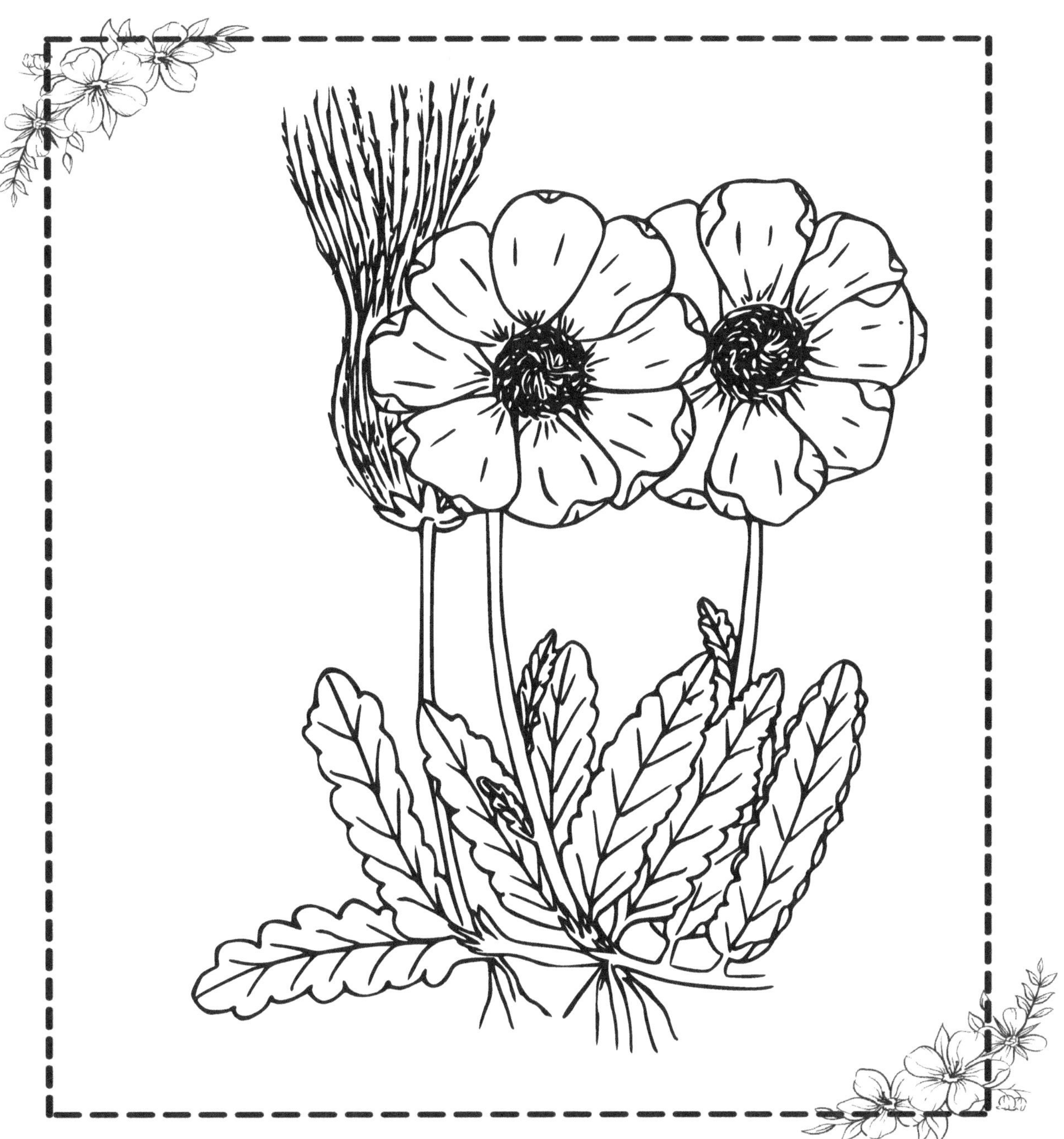

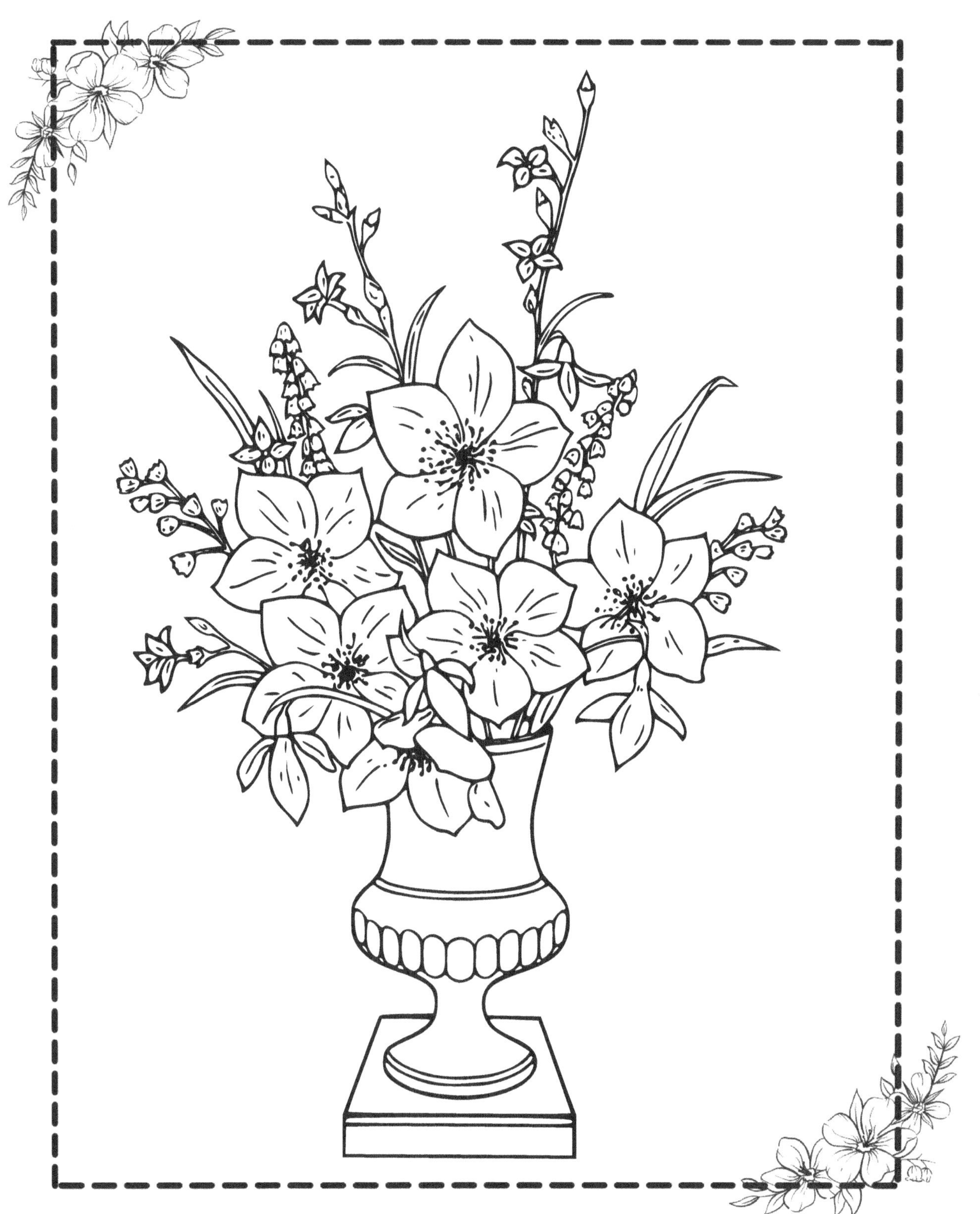

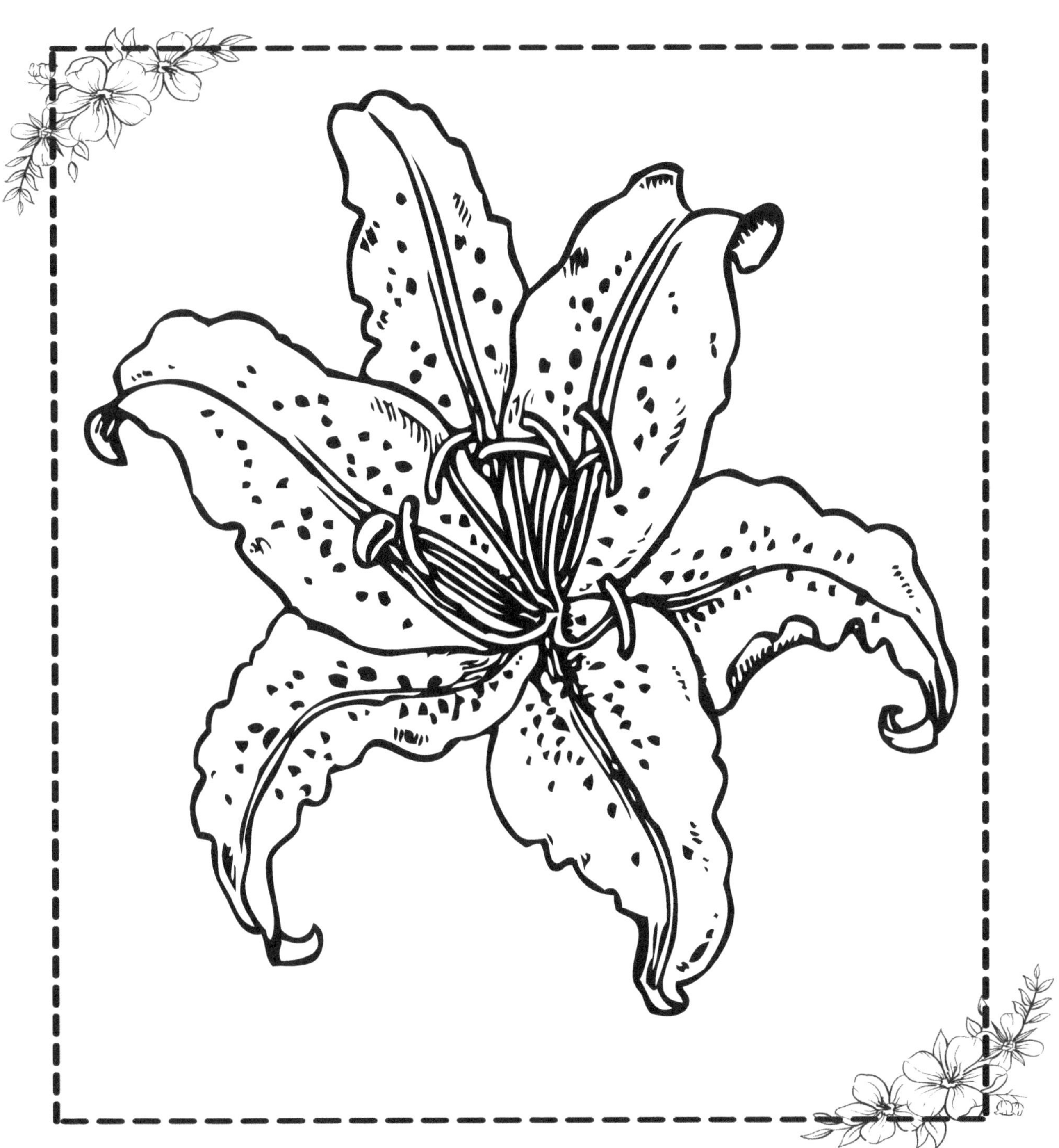

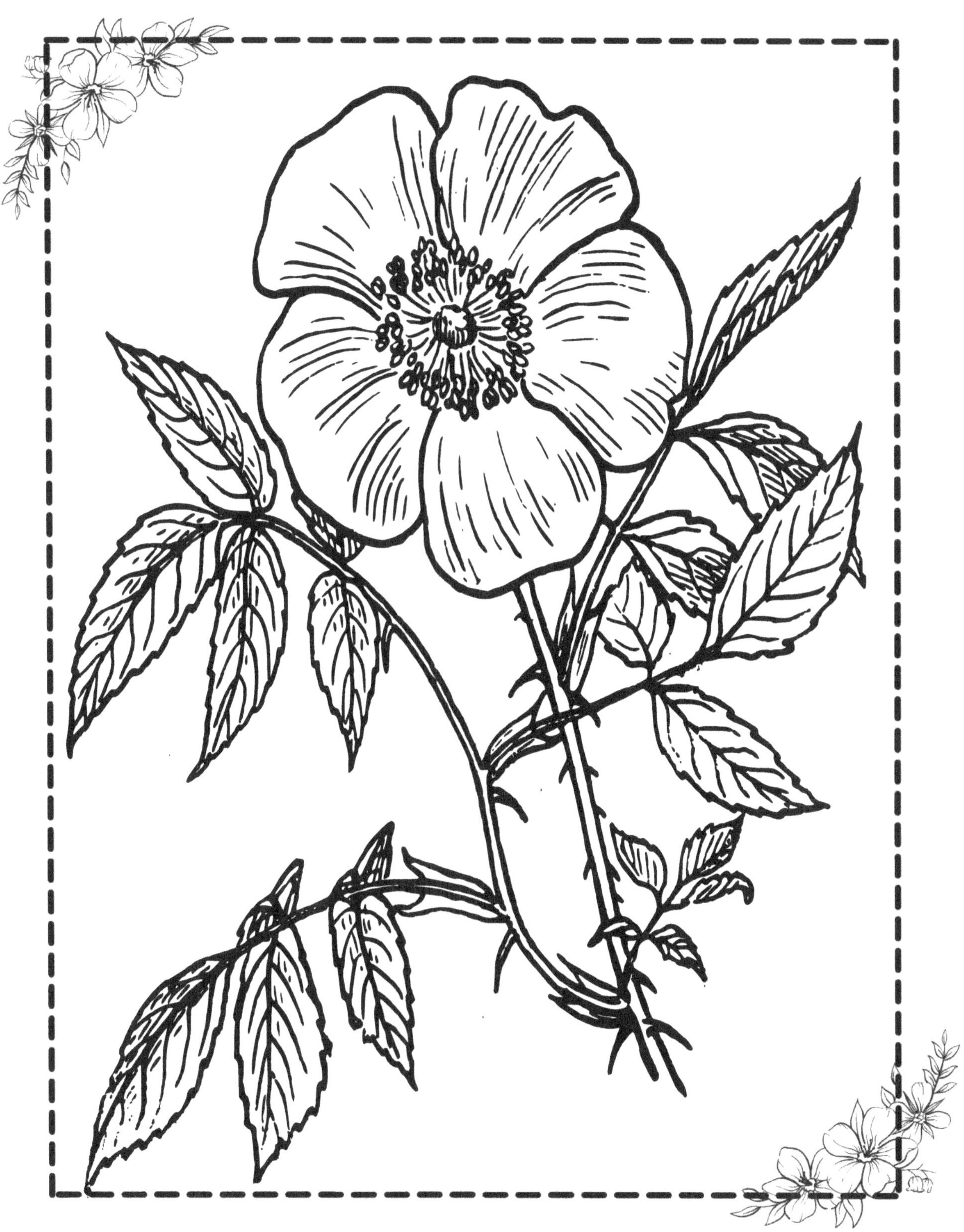

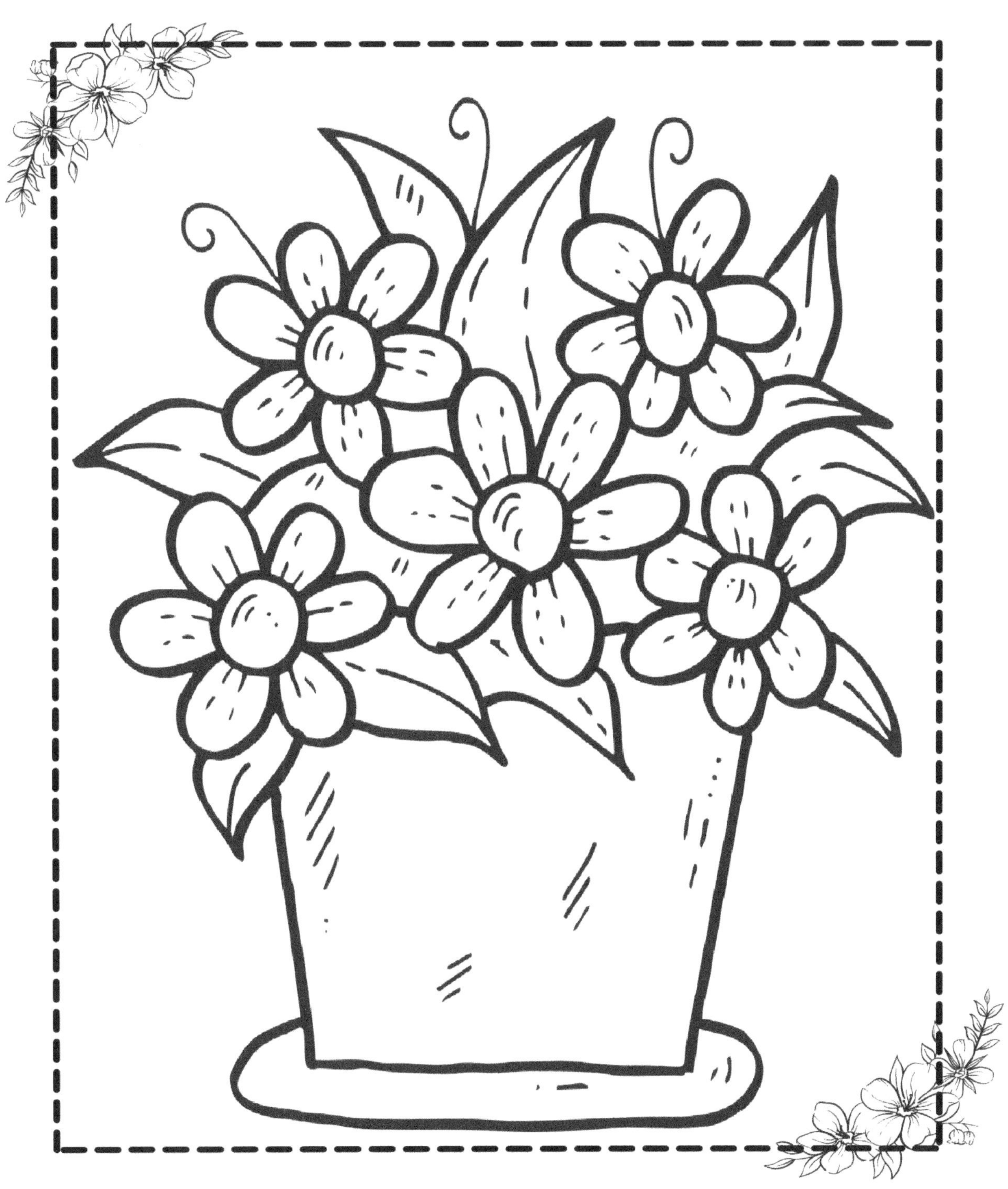

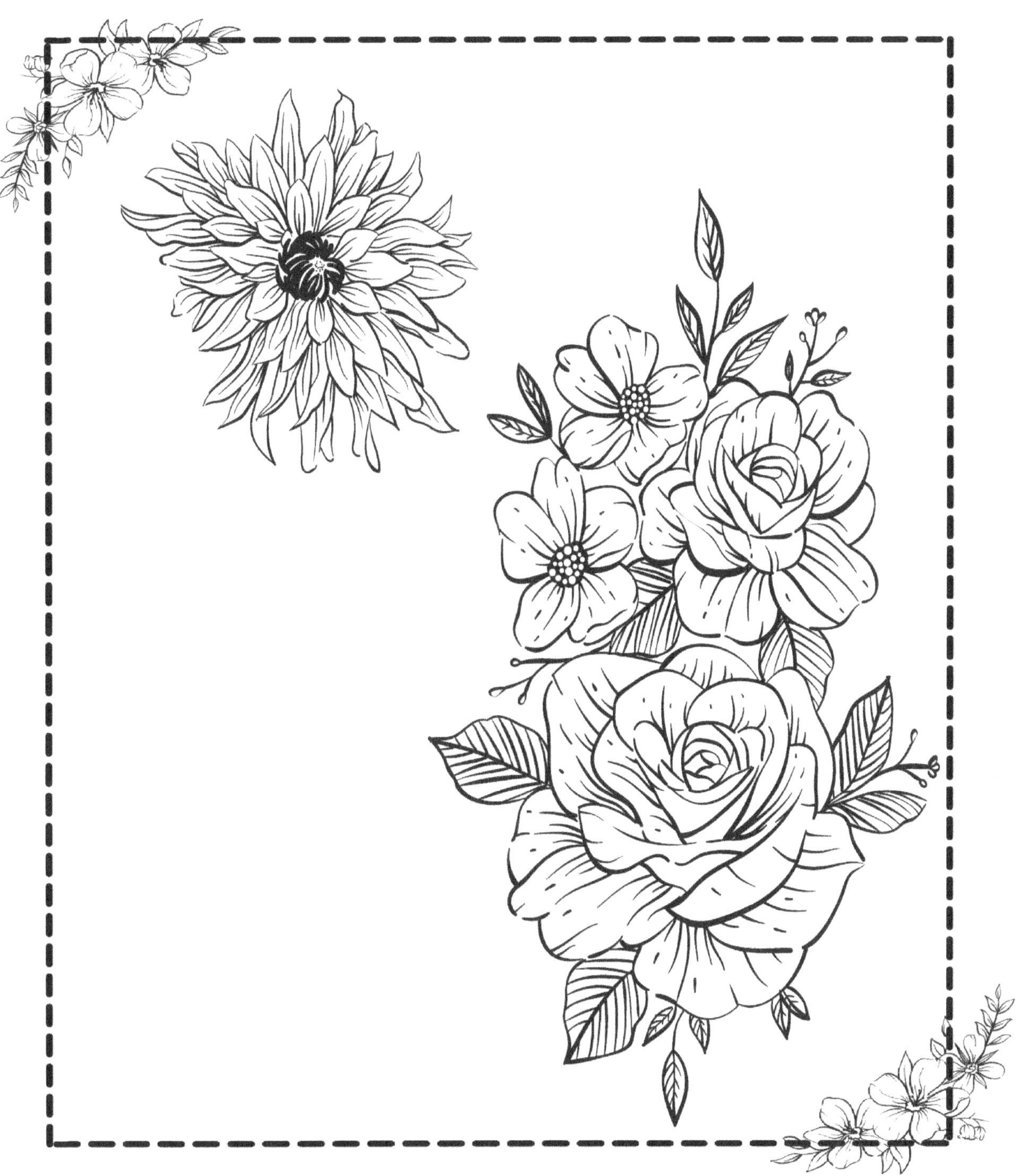

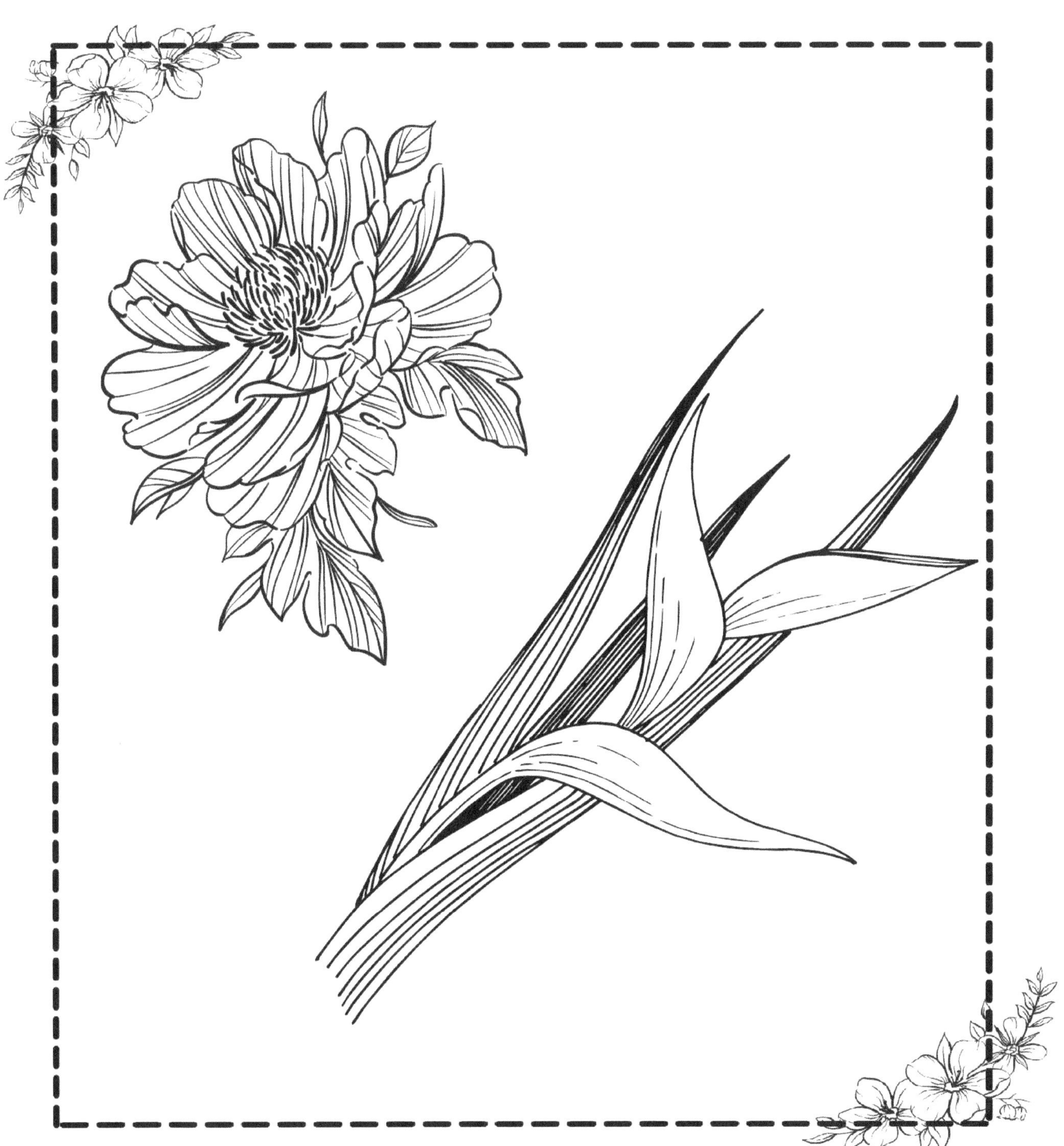

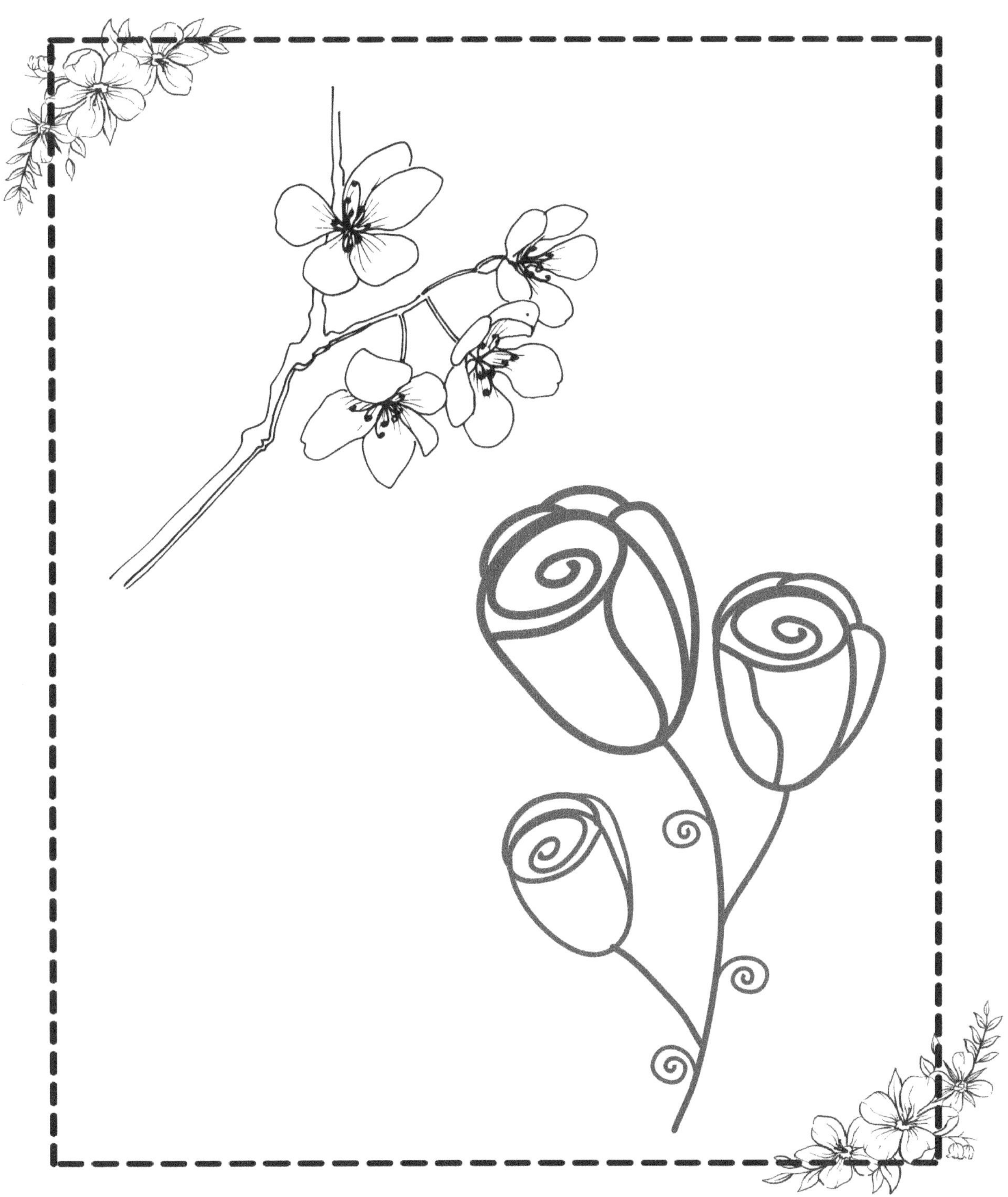

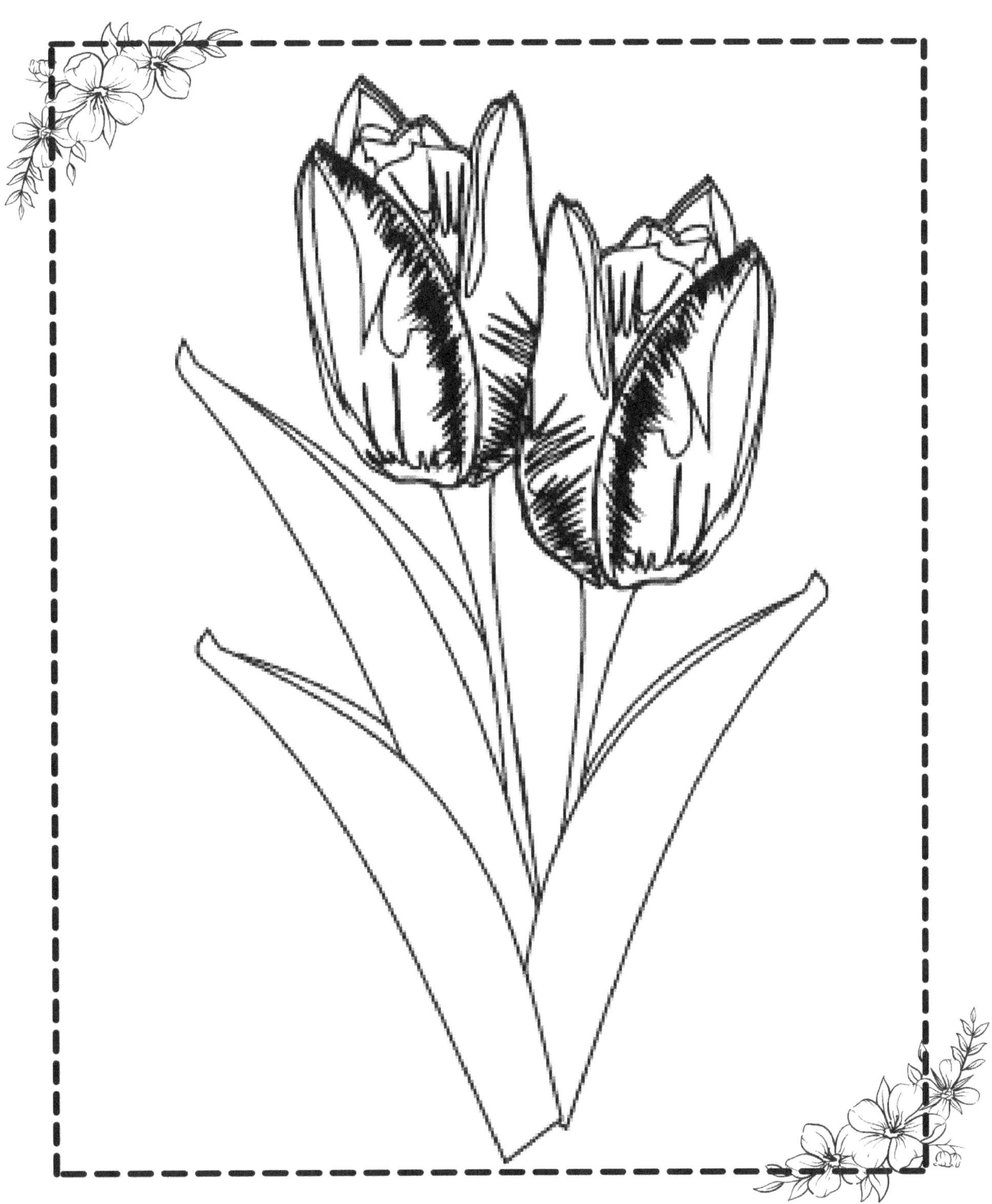

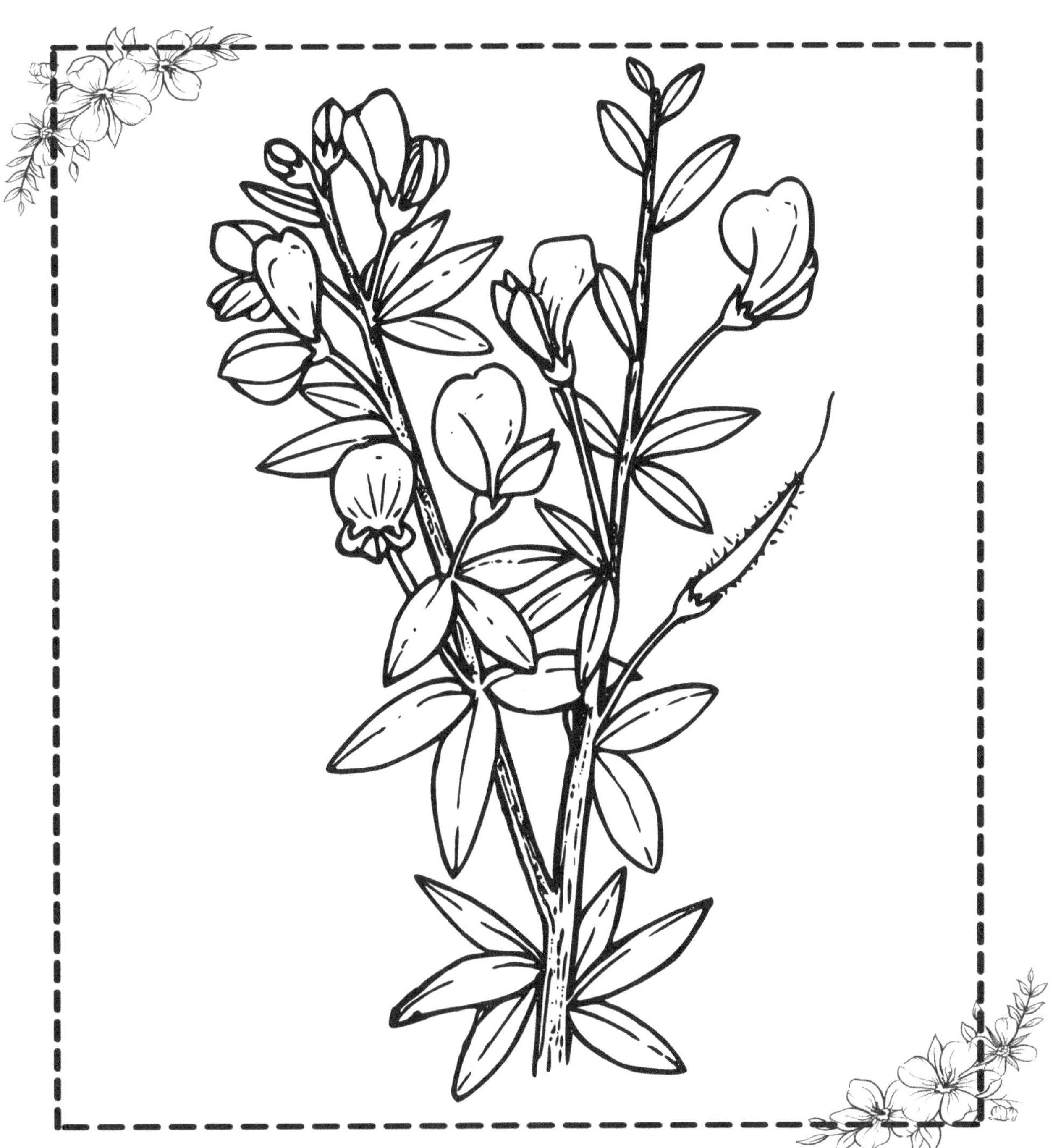

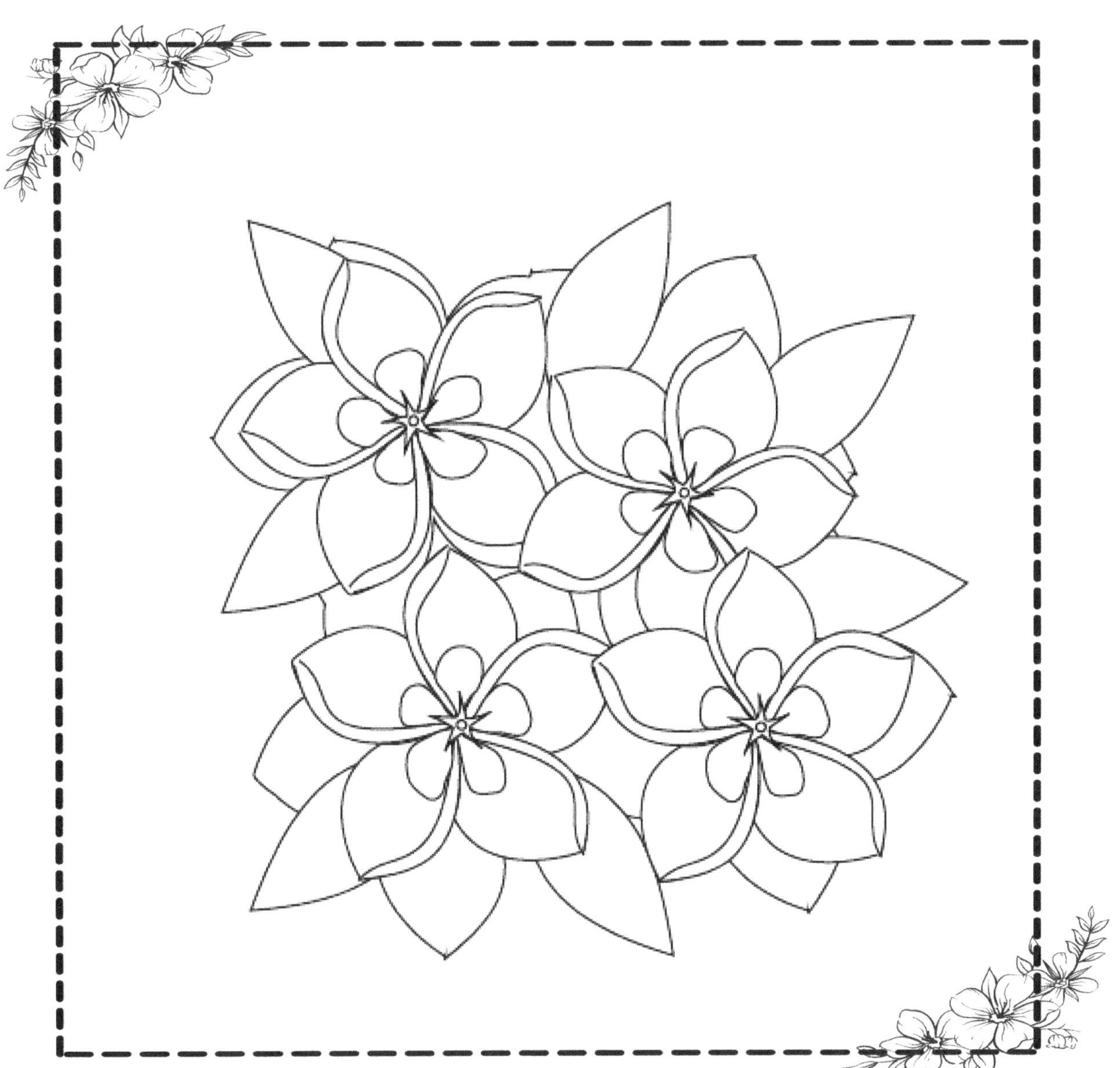

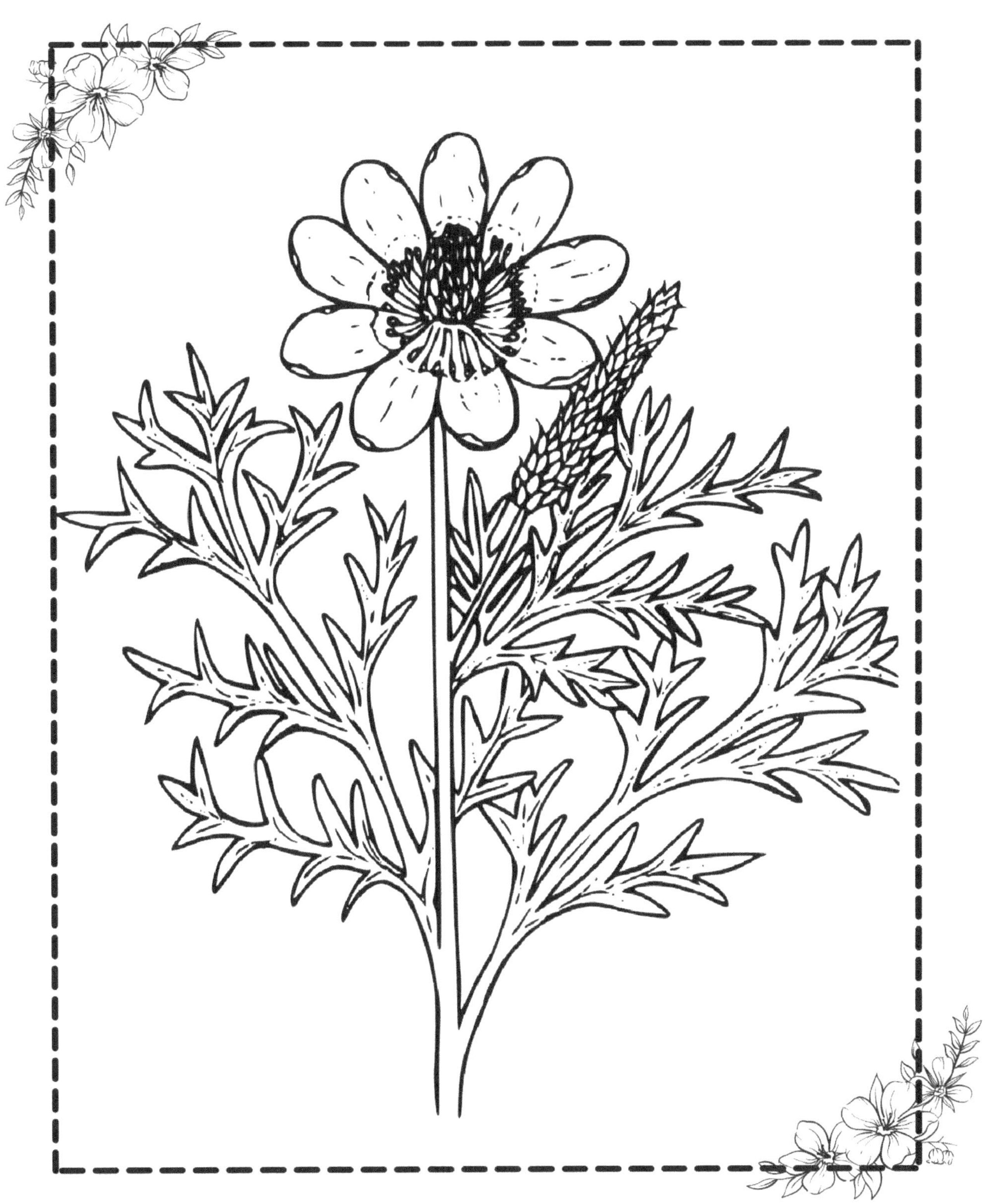

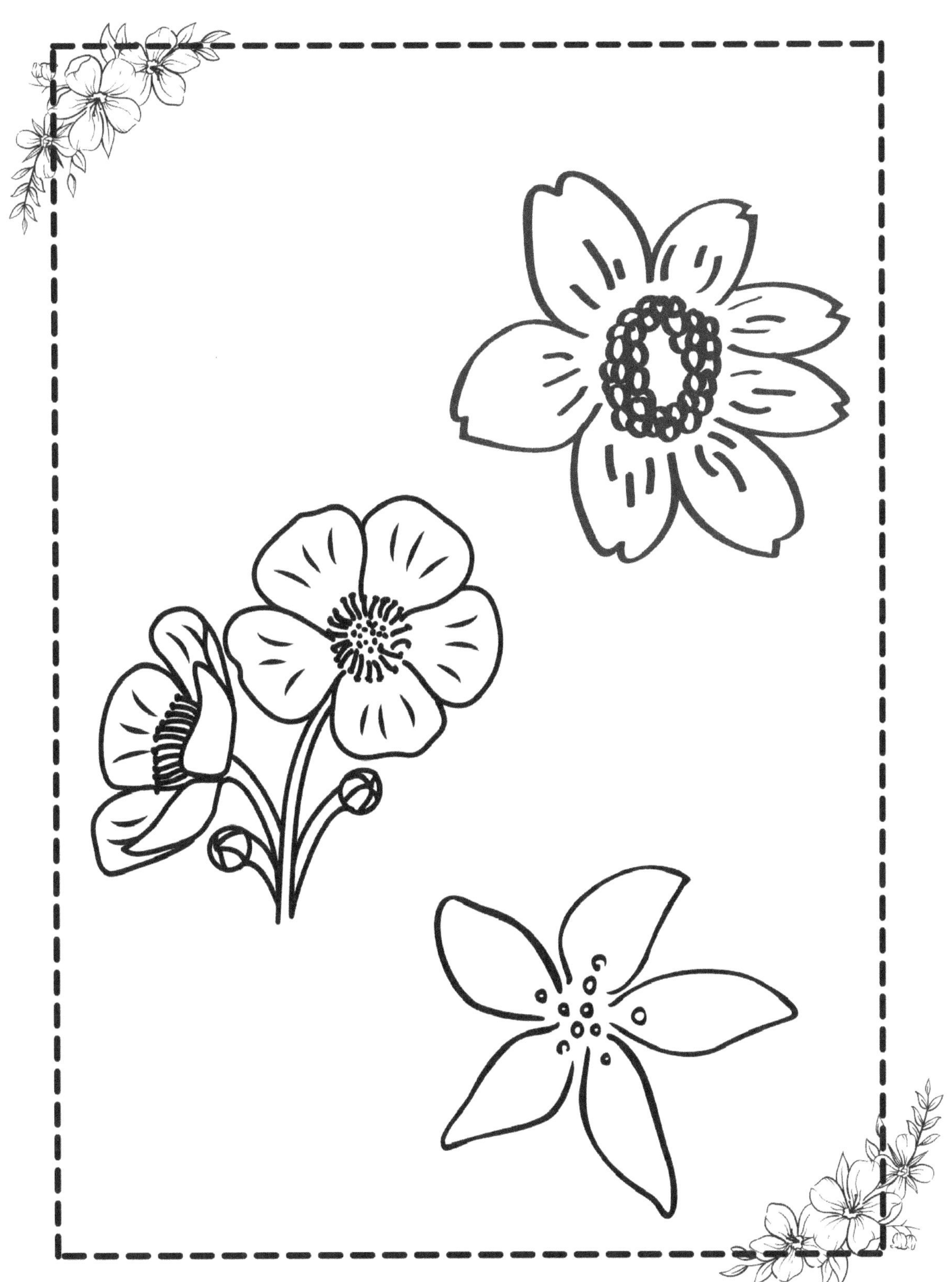

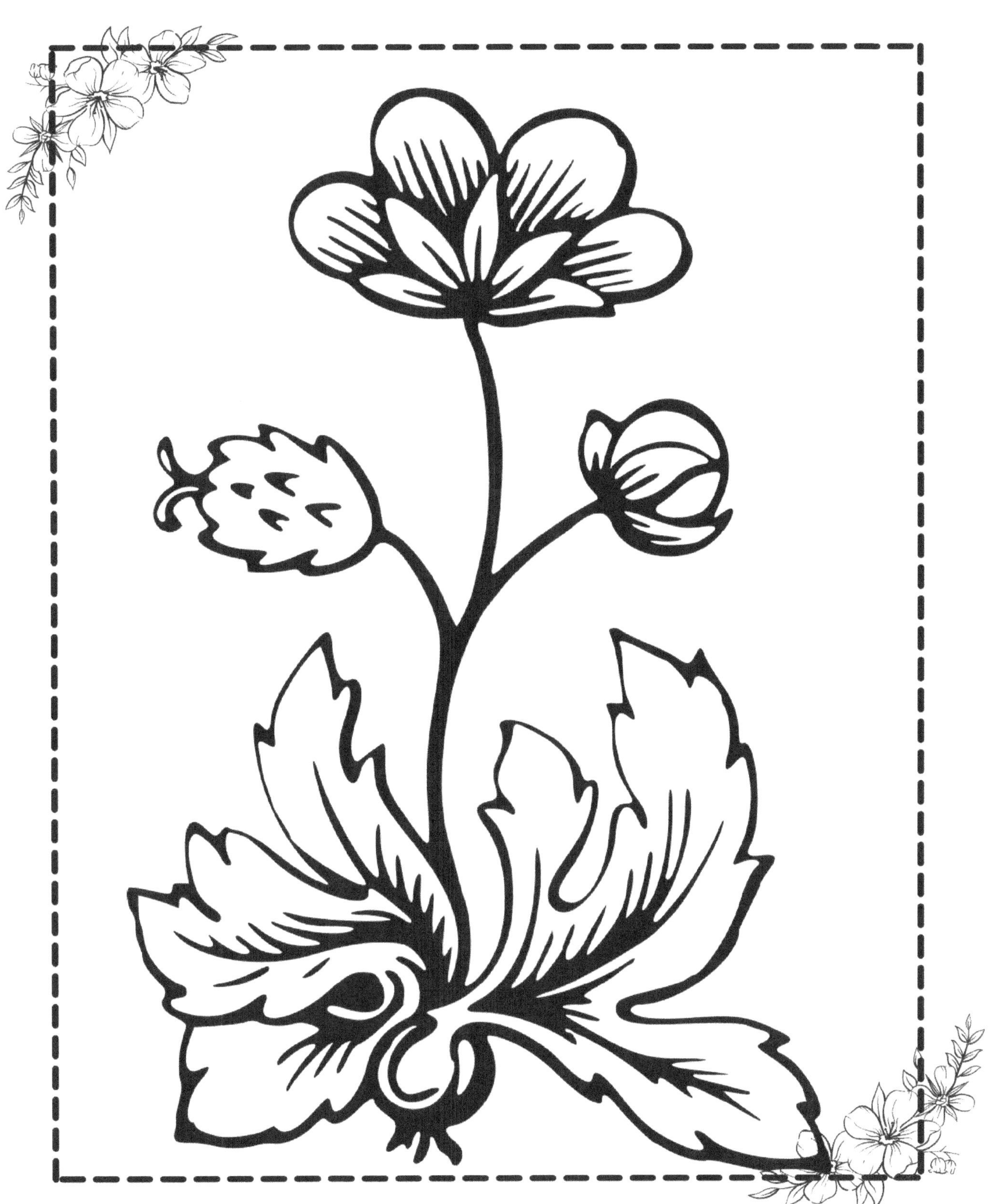

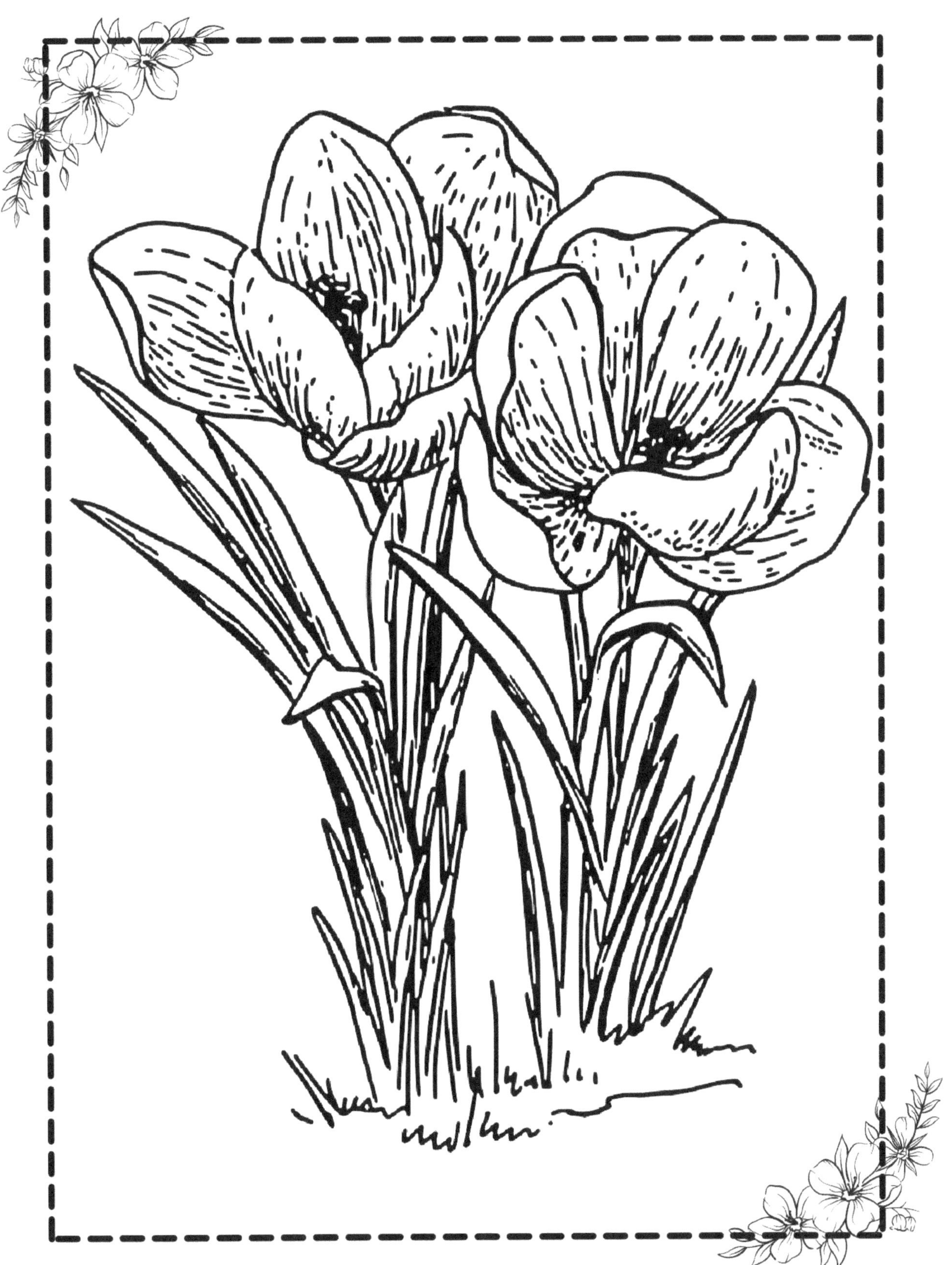

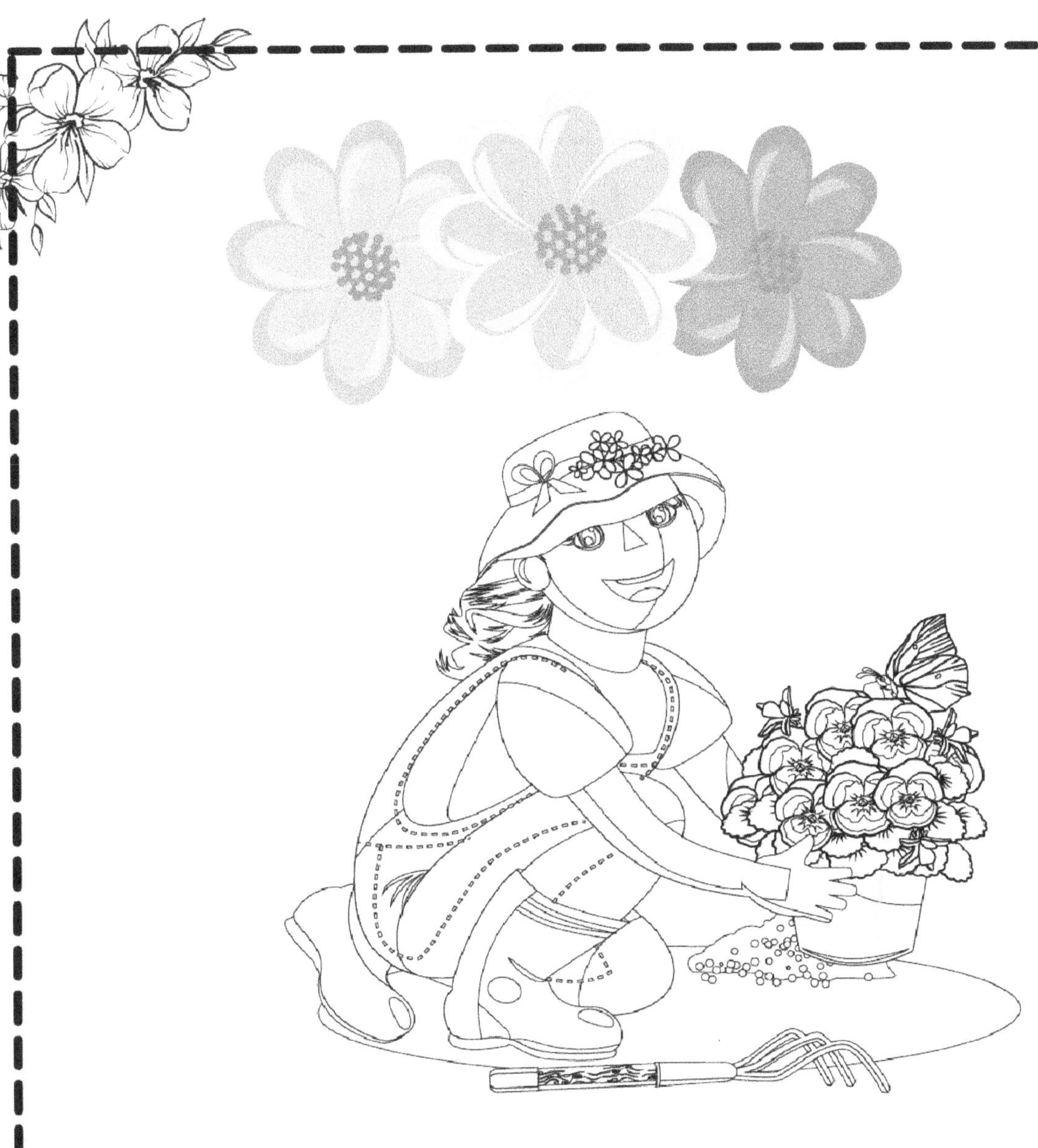

FINISH

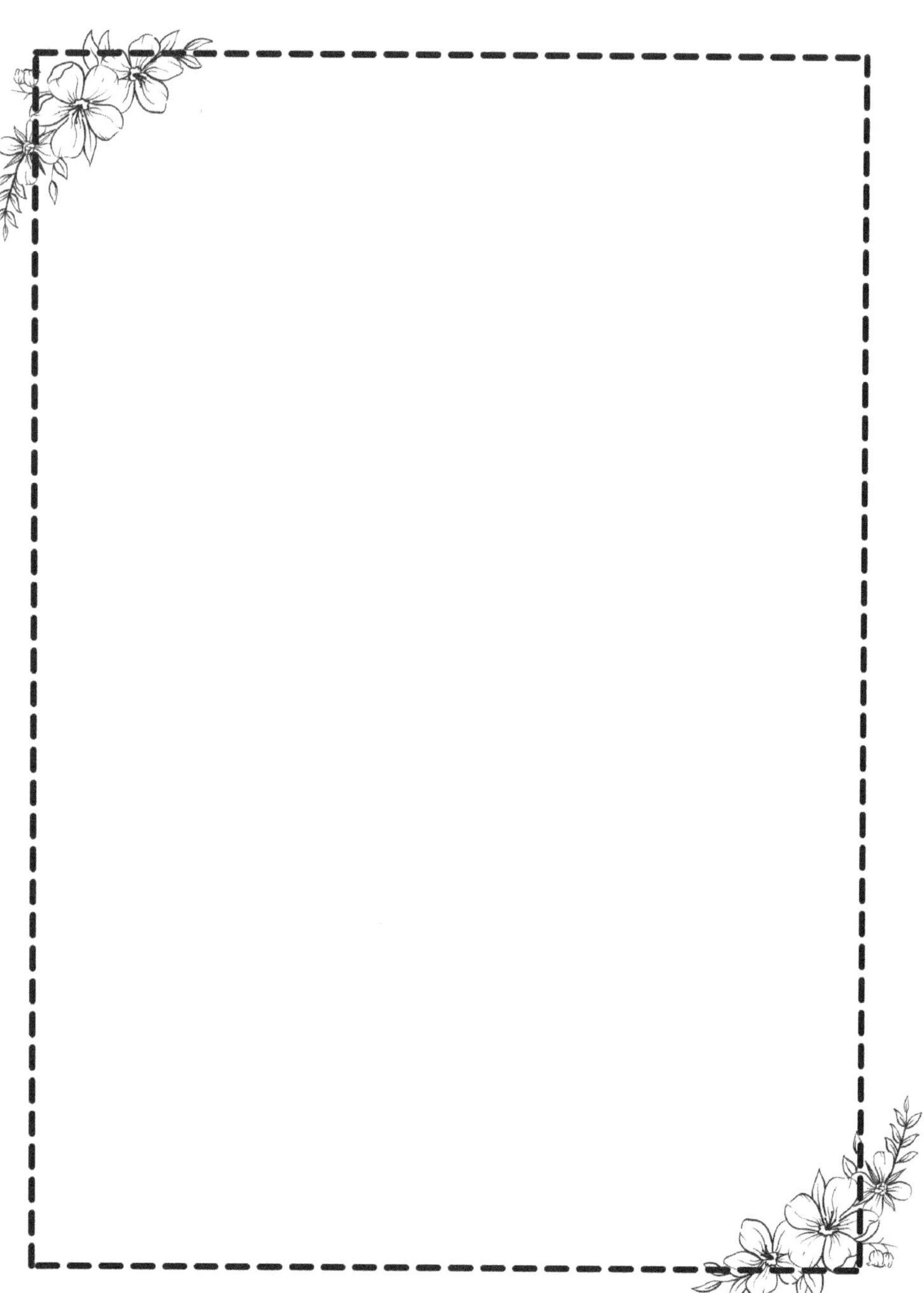